CAKE DECORATING

MITZIE & RAY WILSON

HAMLYN

Produced by New Leaf Productions

Photography by Mick Duff
Design by Jim Wire
Series Editor: Sarah Wallace

First published in 1984 by
Hamlyn Publishing
Astronaut House, Feltham, Middlesex, England

Third impression 1984

ISBN 0 600 20806 0

Printed in Spain

Larsa D. L. TF. 932 – 1984

NOTE

1. Metric and imperial measurements have been calculated separately. Use one set of measurements only as they are not exact equivalents.

2. All spoon measures are level unless otherwise stated.

3. Always pre-heat the oven to the given temperature. Cooking times may vary according to the oven. For fan-assisted ovens cooking times may be shorter, so always follow manufacturers' instructions.

3

CONTENTS

EQUIPMENT 4

BASIC CAKE RECIPES
  Rich Fruit Cake 8
  All-in-one Cake Mix 10
  Whisked Sponge Cake or Swiss Roll 12
  Golden Christmas Cake 13

ICING RECIPES AND TECHNIQUES
  Almond Paste 14
  Royal Icing and How to Royal Ice 16
  Decoration and Gelatine Icing 18
  Glacé and Butter Icing and Rich Butter
    Cream 20

PIPING DESIGNS
  Basic Piping and Decorating 22
  Borders 24
  Run-outs and Bells 26
  Trellis, Basket and Lace Work 28

FLOWERS AND FRILLS
  Piping Roses, Flowers and Leaves 30
  Modelling Roses, Flowers and Leaves 32

Modelling Animals and Figures 34
Making Frills, Flounces and Flowers 36

SPECIAL OCCASION CAKES
  Engagement and Valentine 38
  Wedding 40
  Christening 46
  Novelty Birthday 48
  Coming of Age 54
  Special Celebration 58
  Anniversary 60
  Good Luck and Best Wishes 62
  Moving House or Retirement 64
  Mother's Day and Father's Day 66
  Box and Basket 68
  Easter 70
  Christmas 72

TEMPLATES 78

INDEX 80

ACKNOWLEDGEMENTS 80

EQUIPMENT

Tools of the trade

You will probably already have most of the basic pieces of equipment needed for making and decorating the simplest of cakes – kitchen scales, various-sized bowls and basins, a measuring jug, measuring spoons (particularly useful for accurate measuring of egg albumen and liquid glucose), a nylon sieve, wooden spoon, plastic spatula, pastry brush, rolling pin and several small bowls with airtight seals for mixing coloured icings. Cocktail sticks, an artist's paint brush and a skewer are also useful accessories.

Special icing equipment is required for more skilful designs and it is wise to invest in a good basic kit. Buy the best equipment. Not only will it last longer but you will also be able to extend the range of equipment as and when necessary.

Palette knives A small palette knife is ideal for spreading and smoothing icing onto the sides of cakes and mixing food colourings into icing. A large palette knife mixes icing to a smooth consistency and can sometimes be used for flat icing the top of a cake.

Icing ruler Essential for flat icing the tops of cakes. An ordinary smooth-edged plastic ruler will do. Choose a firm (not flexible) one, at least 30cm/12in, preferably 35cm/14in for icing larger cakes. Steel icing rulers are even better and are available from cake-decorating suppliers.

Icing scrapers Essential for smooth flat icing around the sides of cakes. They are simply pulled around the sides until smooth. Serrated scrapers, also available, give a ridged effect.

Piping nozzles Metal nozzles are strongest and give the best definition. The kind of nozzles needed depends on the icing design. A good basic range is shown on pp.22–3. The easiest way to identify a nozzle is by its number, but since manufacturers vary, always check the design.

Screw-on nozzles For use with nylon icing bags which have a screw connector fitted inside. They will also screw onto their own type of syringe.

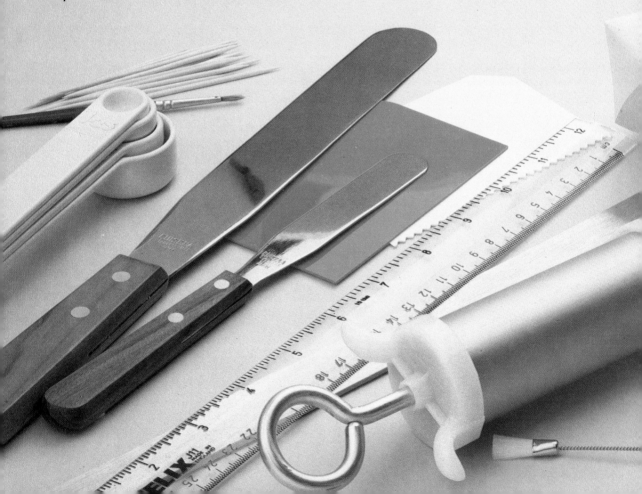

Plain nozzles Nozzles without a screw thread are ideal for use in greaseproof paper icing bags. They can also be used with nylon icing bags which have an adaptor placed inside the bag and a collar which fits over the outside of the bag to screw the nozzle into a secure position. The icing syringe for this type of nozzle also has a collar which screws over the nozzle.

To clean icing nozzles, soak in warm soapy water until icing dissolves away. If any icing remains, use a very small brush, taking care not to harm the shape of the nozzle tip.

Icing syringe Easy to assemble and easy to clean, they allow you to change icing nozzles without emptying the syringe. Many people argue that a paper icing bag allows more fingertip control, and, indeed, a syringe can be uncomfortable over long periods of icing. Use whichever you find easiest. To fill a syringe, place the icing down one side of the tube, fill only half full and gradually press plunger in at an angle to expel air.

Icing bags Nylon or plastic icing bags are clean and convenient. Choose small bags for fine delicate piping and medium bags for piping stars and thicker designs. Large bags are generally too cumbersome for royal icing. Greaseproof paper icing bags will take any nozzle, are simple to use and easy to make (follow directions on p.6). Make up a batch at a time. Very good quality greaseproof paper or baking parchment make stronger bags which can be refilled.

Turntables Not essential since it is possible to ice a stationary cake. But it does help to turn the cake as you decorate, so a turntable is worth investing in, if you intend to do a lot of cake icing. Choose a turntable which revolves smoothly. They can be of heavy metal or plastic and vary in height and price.

Icing nails Useful for making royal iced flowers. A bottle cork pierced onto a skewer works just as well. Cradle, pyramid and basket moulds are also available. These can be piped with royal icing to form given shapes, allowed to dry and then lifted.

Cake markers A great help in marking out accurate patterns on cakes. They are simply positioned on the cake and the design is marked with a pin or dot of icing. Ideal for 'S' or 'C' scrolls, circles, portions and even stars, the marks are then joined up with icing.

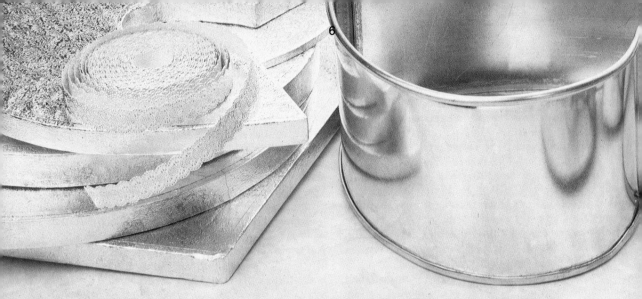

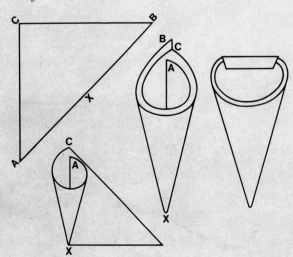

Cake boards

For formal iced cakes the board should be at least 5/8in thick, with a diameter at least 5cm/2in larger than the cake itself, so that there is room for a border of icing around the base of the cake. This also prevents the sides of the cake being knocked, especially during transport. The cake should be placed on the board before covering with almond paste. Thinner boards are useful for sponge or all-in-one birthday or Christmas cakes. For less formal occasions cover a chopping board with kitchen foil or foil wrapping paper.

How to make paper icing bags

Fold a 25cm/10in square of greaseproof paper in half diagonally. Roll point A to come in front of point C. Roll point B to come behind C. Fold down all points to secure the bag. Cut off tip to take a piping nozzle.

★ *Use baking parchment to make stronger bags which can be refilled.*

Choice and preparation of cake tins

A selection of different-sized cake tins will be necessary if you intend to make and decorate a wide variety of cakes. Good tins are expensive, but will last a lifetime. Choose firm metal ones which do not flex easily – or they will distort with oven heat. Try to buy a set of tins which graduate in size at 2.5cm/1in intervals. Three good basic sizes are 15, 20, and 25cm/6, 8 and 10in or 18, 23 and 28cm/7, 9 and 11in which will be sufficient for birthday, celebration and wedding cakes. Round, square, hexagonal and heart-shaped cake tins are available in graduating sizes. Size may vary according to the manufacturer. New metric-sized tins may be slightly larger. Numerals and novelty-shaped tins are sometimes available for hire from cake-decorating suppliers (p.80).

Lining cake tins It is essential to grease and line all cake tins (follow manufacturers' instructions for non-stick tins).

Only the base of shallow round sandwich tins need be lined for whisked sponge cakes and all-in-one cake mixtures. For rich fruit cake mixtures which require long, slow baking the side should also be lined. Use a single thickness of greaseproof paper for the side (a double layer will pucker) and a double thickness for the base. Place the cake tin on a double thickness of greaseproof paper, draw and then cut around the tin. Cut 1 long strip (or 2 smaller ones) 2.5cm/1in higher than the side of the tin to reach right around the tin plus 2.5cm/1 in to overlap. Fold the bottom edge up about 2cm/3/4in and make slanting cuts every 2cm/3/4in into the fold. Grease the tin with melted fat or oil, place 1 circle of greaseproof paper in the base, fit the strip against the side and place the remaining circle of greaseproof paper in the base to cover up slashed edges. Grease the greaseproof paper with more melted fat or oil.

For rich fruit cakes which require long cooking times stand the cake tin on a baking sheet lined with a double thickness of brown paper and tie a strip of double-thickness brown paper around the outside of the tin to prevent overcooking of edges.

To line a square tin follow instructions as for the round tin, but fold the paper sharply into each corner of the tin.

To line a Swiss roll tin or cakes baked in long, shallow oblong tins, it is wise to grease and line the cake tin for easy removal. Cut a piece of grease-proof paper about 4cm/1½in larger than tin all the way around. Place the tin on the paper, mark the corners and cut to each corner of the tin. Grease the tin, put in the paper, overlapping the corners to give neat sharp angles. Grease again.

To line a loaf tin grease and line in the same way as the Swiss roll tin, but cut the paper at least 15cm/6in larger than the top of the tin.

BASIC CAKE RECIPES

RICH FRUIT CAKE

Rich, dark and moist, this traditional recipe cuts well without crumbling. Use this cake for wedding, birthday, Christmas and all royal iced cakes. The cakes are scaled to vary in depth, from 6.5cm/2½in for smaller cakes up to 7.5cm/3in for larger cakes. This gives a tiered wedding cake a balanced look.

For best results weigh the eggs without their shells (each egg will weigh approximately 50g/2 oz). You need an equal weight of butter, sugar and eggs.

Heat the oven to 150°C/300°F/Gas 2. Grease and line cake tins (pp.6–7). Halve, wash and dry the cherries and place in a large bowl. Weigh and add the flour, currants, sultanas, raisins, mixed peel and nuts. Mix together with 1 tsp–1 tbsp of ground mixed spice – depending on the size of the cake. In another large bowl cream the butter and sugar until light and fluffy. Gradually add the whisked eggs, beating well after each addition. Add a little of the flour and fruit if the mixture begins to curdle. Add essences and a little gravy browning to give a darker mixture if required. Mix in the rest of the fruit and flour mixture. Put into a prepared tin and level the top with the back of a spoon. Put the tin on a double sheet of brown paper on a baking tray and put in the oven, reducing temperature to 140°C/275°F/Gas 1. Cook for the time stated in the chart. When cooked, the cake should feel firm. Remove from the oven and allow to cool in the tin. When quite cold remove from the tin (leave the greaseproof paper on as this helps to keep the cake moist), turn the cake upside down and wrap in greaseproof paper then loosely in polythene. Keep in a cool, dry, dark place. The cake improves with keeping. To increase the keeping time and to improve flavour pierce the top of the cake with a skewer and spoon over a little brandy, sherry or rum. The cake is at its best 4 months after baking.

NOTE
1. Check the cake about 30 minutes before the end of the cooking time.
2. Use 1 tsp–1 tbsp of any or all of the following essences or flavourings – vanilla, rum, almond, lemon, orange, ground mixed spice, brandy or sherry. Brandy is best added after the cake is cooked. The cake rises 1cm/½in when cooked.
3. To store an uncut tier of wedding cake, place in a large cardboard box and keep in a cool, dry place. Do not wrap or seal in a tin or polythene box. We have found from experience that a cake can be kept in this way for up to 2 years.
4. To cut a square or round cake follow the diagrams shown here. Cut the cake in half, then cut into 5cm/2in sections. Cut each section into 1cm/½in slices.
5. For heart-shaped tins, use the recipe for the equivalent-sized square tin. For horseshoe-shaped tins, use the recipe for a round tin 5cm/2in smaller than the horseshoe equivalent.

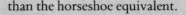

Rich fruit cake chart

METRIC

Round tin	15cm	18cm	20cm	23cm	25cm	28cm	30cm	
Square tin	12.5cm	15cm	18cm	20cm	23cm	25cm	28cm	30cm
★glacé cherries	65g	75g	100g	150g	200g	250g	350g	375g
plain flour	175g	200g	250g	300g	450g	600g	725g	825g
currants	150g	175g	225g	275g	400g	525g	675g	750g
sultanas	200g	250g	350g	425g	600g	800g	1kg	1.125kg
raisins	75g	75g	100g	150g	200g	275g	350g	400g
★mixed peel	50g	50g	50g	75g	100g	150g	175g	200g
★chopped nuts	25g	25g	50g	75g	75g	100g	175g	175g
butter	150g	175g	225g	275g	400g	525g	675g	750g
caster sugar	150g	175g	225g	275g	400g	525g	675g	750g
weight of eggs	150g	175g	225g	275g	400g	525g	675g	750g

IMPERIAL

Round tin	6in	7in	8in	9in	10in	11in	12in	
Square tin	5in	6in	7in	8in	9in	10in	11in	12in
★glacé cherries	2½ oz	3 oz	4 oz	5 oz	7 oz	9 oz	12 oz	13 oz
plain flour	6 oz	7 oz	9 oz	11 oz	1 lb	1 lb 5 oz	1 lb 10 oz	1 lb 13 oz
currants	5 oz	6 oz	8 oz	10 oz	14 oz	1 lb 3 oz	1 lb 8 oz	1 lb 11 oz
sultanas	7½ oz	9 oz	12 oz	15 oz	1 lb 5 oz	1 lb 12 oz	2 lb 4 oz	2 lb 8 oz
raisins	2½ oz	3 oz	4 oz	5 oz	7 oz	10 oz	12 oz	14 oz
★mixed peel	2 oz	2 oz	2 oz	3 oz	4 oz	5 oz	6 oz	7 oz
★chopped nuts	1 oz	1 oz	2 oz	3 oz	3 oz	4 oz	6 oz	6 oz
butter	5 oz	6 oz	8 oz	10 oz	14 oz	1 lb 3 oz	1 lb 8 oz	1 lb 11 oz
caster sugar	5 oz	6 oz	8 oz	10 oz	14 oz	1 lb 3 oz	1 lb 8 oz	1 lb 11 oz
weight of eggs	5 oz	6 oz	8 oz	10 oz	14 oz	1 lb 3 oz	1 lb 8 oz	1 lb 11 oz
cooking time (hours)	3¾	3¾	4	4½	4½	5	5	5

★ *If one of these 3 ingredients is not required, add the extra weight of one of the others.*

ALL-IN-ONE CAKE MIX

This quickly made cake is ideal for novelty cakes and keeps well for 1 week in a tin, up to 2 weeks covered in icing, or frozen for up to 2 months. The cake is firm enough to cut into any shape, yet is moist and crumbly and can be filled with jam, cream or butter icing.

Heat the oven to 180°C/350°F/Gas 4. Brush baking tins or basins with melted fat or oil and line bases with greased greaseproof paper.

Put the margarine, sugar, eggs, sifted flour, baking powder and flavourings in a mixing bowl.

Mix together with a wooden spoon, then beat for 2–3 minutes until the mixture is smooth and glossy. (This will only take 1–2 minutes in an electric mixer, or between 30 seconds and 1 minute in a food processor.) Put the mixture into a prepared tin, level the top with the back of a spoon and bake in the centre of the oven for the required time. Test the cake by pressing with your fingers. If cooked, the cake should spring back and have just begun to shrink from the sides of the tin. Allow to cool for 5 minutes before loosening the sides of the cake from the tin. Turn out onto a wire rack.

All-in-one cake chart

Basic recipe	Cake tin size	Approx. cooking time
100g/4 oz soft tub margarine (chilled)	two 18cm/7in sandwich tins	25–30 minutes
	one 20cm/8in sandwich tin	30–35 minutes
100g/4 oz caster sugar	one 18cm/7in deep square tin	35–40 minutes
two size 2 eggs	one 20cm/8in shallow square tin	25–30 minutes
100g/4 oz self-raising flour	one ½kg/1 lb loaf tin – omit	45–50 minutes
1 tsp baking powder	baking powder	
Flavourings	one 900ml/1½ pint basin – omit	50 minutes–1 hour
4 drops vanilla essence	baking powder	
4 tsp cocoa	one 20cm/8in ring mould	35–40 minutes
2 tsp lemon or orange rind		
2 tsp instant coffee		
175g/6 oz soft tub margarine (chilled)	two 20cm/8in sandwich tins	35–40 minutes
	two 23cm/9in sandwich tins	25 minutes
175g/6 oz caster sugar	one 15cm/6in deep cake tin	45–50 minutes
three size 2 eggs	one 18cm/7in deep square tin	45–50 minutes
175g/6 oz self-raising flour	one 28 × 18cm/11 × 7in	35–40 minutes
1½ tsp baking powder	Swiss roll tin	
Flavourings	1.2 litre/2 pint basin – omit	1¼–1½ hours
6 drops vanilla essence	baking powder	
2 tbsp cocoa		
1 tbsp lemon or orange rind		
1 tbsp instant coffee		
225g/8 oz soft tub margarine (chilled)	one 23cm/9in round tin – omit baking powder	1 hour
225g/8 oz caster sugar	one 23cm/9in square tin – omit baking powder	1 hour
four size 2 eggs		
225g/8oz self-raising flour	one 29 × 22cm/11½ × 8½in	40 minutes
2 tsp baking powder	Swiss roll tin	
Flavourings		
8 drops vanilla essence		
4 tbsp cocoa		
2 tbsp lemon or orange rind		
2 tbsp instant coffee		

WHISKED SPONGE CAKE OR SWISS ROLL

This light fluffy cake is ideal for afternoon tea filled with cream, fruit or butter icing. It does not keep well and is best eaten the day it is made or frozen for up to 2 months.

Prepare oven (see chart). Grease and line the cake tin (p.7) and dust sponge tin lightly with flour. Put the eggs and sugar in a bowl and whisk until the mixture becomes thick and frothy like a mousse texture. The mixture should be thick enough to leave a definite trail when lifted. It is easiest to use an electric mixer, but if using a hand whisk, put the bowl over a saucepan of hot water (the bowl must not touch the water or the eggs will cook) or heat the sugar on a plate in the oven until warm. Sift the flour and baking powder together. Carefully fold into the egg mixture using a large metal spoon (a draining spoon is particularly useful). Be careful not to knock out all the air and cut through the mixture until all the flour is incorporated. Pour into a prepared tin. Shake the tin gently to level the mixture. Bake in the centre of the oven (see chart).

Sponge cake – remove from the tin and leave to cool on a wire rack. Swiss roll – while the cake is baking cut a piece of greaseproof paper 2.5cm/1in bigger all round than the tin. Sprinkle with caster sugar. Invert cake onto paper, quickly loosen and remove paper from the sides and bottom of the cake. Trim off edges with a sharp knife. Make a cut halfway through the thickness of the cake 2.5cm/1in from and parallel with the end from which cake will be rolled.

Spread the cake with jam, if using. (If filling with cream or butter icing roll the cake with greaseproof paper inside. When cool, unroll, remove paper and fill.) To roll – press the half-cut edge down and, using the paper, roll up the cake tightly. Hold the cake for a moment with the wrapped greaseproof paper inside to allow the cake to set. Leave to cool on a wire rack.

Whisked sponge cake and Swiss roll chart

Basic recipe	Tin size	Temperature	Time
2 eggs 50g/2 oz caster sugar 50g/2 oz plain flour ½ tsp baking powder	two 18cm/7in sandwich tins one 20cm/8in sandwich tin one 28 × 18cm/11 × 7in Swiss roll tin	180°C/350°F/Gas 4 180°C/350°F/Gas 4 200°C/400°F/Gas 6	15–20 minutes 20–25 minutes 5–8 minutes
3 eggs 75g/3 oz caster sugar 75g/3oz plain flour ½ tsp baking powder	two 20cm/8in sandwich tins one 20cm/8in deep round tin one 32 × 22cm/12½ × 8½in Swiss roll tin	180°C/350°F/Gas 4 180°C/350°F/Gas 4 200°C/400°F/Gas 6	20–25 minutes 35–40 minutes 8—10 minutes

Flavourings
  Chocolate: replace 25g/1 oz flour with 25g/1 oz cocoa.
  Coffee: add 1–2 tsp instant coffee to the egg-and-sugar-stage mixture.
  Orange/lemon: add 1–2 tsp grated rind.

GOLDEN CHRISTMAS CAKE

This is my favourite Christmas cake recipe from *Family Circle* magazine. Extra moist and crumbly, this cake will keep for up to 3 weeks in a tin. Or you can wrap the cake in a double layer of cling film and store in the fridge for 6 weeks or for 3 months in the freezer. To make an 18cm/7in square or 20cm/8in round cake you need:

100g/4 oz dried apricots
100g/4 oz marzipan
175g/6 oz butter
175g/6 oz caster sugar
3 eggs
100g/4 oz glacé cherries, halved
100g/4 oz walnuts, chopped
rind and juice of 1 large orange
225g/8 oz sultanas
225g/8 oz wholewheat flour
1 tsp baking powder
2 tsp ground cinnamon

Heat the oven to 160°C/325°F/Gas 3. Grease and line the cake tin (pp.6–7). Snip the apricots into quarters, place in a basin and cover with boiling water. Roll the marzipan into marble-sized balls. Cream the butter and sugar until light and fluffy. Beat eggs, add a little at a time and beat well after each addition. Drain the apricots well and stir in with the cherries, walnuts, marzipan, orange rind, 150ml/¼ pint orange juice (make up with apricot liquor if necessary) and sultanas. Mix well. Sift the flour, baking powder and cinnamon together and fold into the mixture (adding the pieces of bran from the sieve).

Place the mixture in a tin and smooth the top with the back of a spoon. Place the tin on a baking sheet and bake in the centre of the oven for 1 hour. Reduce heat to 150°C/300°F/Gas 2 and cook for a further 1 hour 15 minutes–1 hour 30 minutes. If cooked, the cake will spring back and have begun to shrink from the sides of the tin. Leave to cool, then turn out and store in a tin. Almond paste, ice and decorate as desired.

ICING RECIPES AND TECHNIQUES

ALMOND PASTE

Almond paste is used as a base cover for fruit cakes before coating with royal or decoration icing.

350g/12 oz ground almonds
175g/6 oz caster sugar
175g/6 oz icing sugar
1 large egg or 2–3 yolks
few drops of almond flavouring

OR ECONOMICAL RECIPE
225g/8 oz ground almonds
225g/8 oz caster sugar
225g/8 oz icing sugar
1 large egg or 2–3 yolks
few drops of almond flavouring

Mix the dry ingredients together. Beat the egg with the flavouring and add to the dry mixture. Stir to a firm rollable paste. For a whiter paste use egg whites only (2–3) which makes the paste more suitable for modelling.

These ingredients are sufficient to cover a 20cm/8in round or 18cm/7in square cake. Follow the chart for other sizes and adjust recipe quantities accordingly.

Square	Round	Almond paste
12.5cm/5in	15cm/6in	350g/12 oz
15cm/6in	18cm/7in	550g/1 lb 4 oz
18cm/7in	20cm/8in	675g/1½lb
20cm/8in	23cm/9in	675g/1½ lb
23cm/9in	25cm/10in	900g/2 lb
25cm/10in	28cm/11in	1kg/2 lb
28cm/11in	30cm/12in	1.125kg/2½ lb
30cm/12in		1.5kg/3 lb

Prepare the cake by levelling the top if necessary. To enable the almond paste to stick to the cake, beat 1 egg white with 2 tsp brandy. Brush over the top and sides of the cake. Alternatively, brush the cake with warm, sieved apricot jam. Dust work surface with icing sugar, roll half the almond paste 2.5cm/1in larger than the top of the cake. Place the cake upside down on the almond paste. Using a small palette knife, draw up the edge of the paste, flattening against each side of the cake. Trim off any surplus and smooth evenly. This method gives a very smooth top, but for large cakes (25–30cm/ 10–12in) it is easier to lift the almond paste onto the top of the cake. Roll lightly with a rolling pin and trim sides. Place the cake on the cake board.

Cut 2 pieces of string or thread, one the exact circumference of the cake, the other the exact height. Cut the remaining almond paste in half, work into 2 sausage shapes and roll each into an oblong. Trim to the height and half the circumference of the cake using the string as a guide. Carefully wrap each piece around the cake, pressing firmly onto the side. Smooth top and side joins together with a knife. For a square cake cut 4 oblongs the exact length and height of each side, smooth the joins with a knife and press lightly to give neat corners.

Leave for 24 hours to dry. Wedding cakes should be allowed to dry for up to 1 week before icing, to avoid the almond oil staining the icing should the wedding cake be stored after the wedding.

ROYAL ICING

2½ tsp powdered egg white (albumen)
4 tbsp cold water
450g/1 lb icing sugar
glycerine (optional)

OR
2 large egg whites
450g/1 lb icing sugar
glycerine (optional)

It is important to make sure the mixing bowl and beaters are spotlessly clean and grease-free. Put the albumen or egg whites in a bowl and whisk well with a fork. Gradually beat in the icing sugar until the mixture becomes very white and smooth. It is important to beat the icing for a long time to get the right consistency – even for up to 20 minutes. (Or use an electric mixer with the beater attachment. Beat on a slow speed for 10–15 minutes. Cover the mixer with a clean teacloth to prevent the icing sugar spreading everywhere.) Run a palette knife through the icing. If it is the correct consistency, the knife will leave a clear smooth road through the icing and the mixture will stand in a peak. Add the glycerine and beat for another minute.

Keep the basin covered while the icing is being used, either with lid or a slightly damp cloth. Store in an airtight container in a cool place for up to 10 days. The icing will need re-mixing for 1–2 minutes to restore consistency.

The quantity required for covering and decorating a cake is as follows.

Square	Round	Icing sugar
12.5cm/5in	15cm/6in	675g/1½ lb
15cm/6in	18cm/7in	900g/2 lb
18cm/7in	20cm/8in	1.125kg/2½ lb
20cm/8in	23cm/9in	1.5kg/3 lb
23cm/9in	25cm/10in	1.6kg/3½lb
25cm/10in	28cm/11in	1.6kg/3½ lb
28cm/11in	30cm/12in	2kg/4½ lb
30cm/12in		2kg/4½ lb

Powdered egg albumen gives excellent results and is available from cake decorating suppliers.

Add 1 tsp glycerine to prevent the icing from becoming too hard to cut. Do not add glycerine for icing the base tier of a wedding cake or for piping flowers or run-outs.

HOW TO ROYAL ICE

Follow the recipe chart for the quantities required.
To ice side A flat side scraper is essential for professional smooth sides. Using a small palette knife, spread plenty of icing onto the side of the cake, working backwards and forwards with the knife to apply evenly and help remove any air bubbles. For round cakes – place your arm around the back of the cake and as far forward to the front as possible, so that you can sweep the scraper all the way around without stopping. Place the side scraper upright against the side of the cake and scrape lightly all the way around in one sure movement. Draw off the scraper at an angle so the join is hardly noticeable. If using a turntable (you may find this easier particularly for larger cakes), hold the scraper to the side of the cake, pass the other hand under and around the turntable and revolve the turntable quite quickly and smoothly in one revolution, keeping the scraper *still* against the cake. Scrape off the surplus royal icing from the top edge with a small palette knife. Wipe the cake board. Leave to dry for 2–3 hours or overnight before icing the top.

To ice top For the base tier of a wedding cake which must support other tiers, do not add glycerine to the icing. Spread the icing on top of the cake with a small palette knife, working backwards and forwards across the cake. Hold a metal or firm plastic ruler at an angle of about 30° and, with a straight firm movement, draw the ruler towards you across the cake. Take care not to press too hard or the icing will be too thin. Hold a clean palette knife against the side of the cake and carefully scrape off the surplus icing. Leave to dry for at least 1 day before piping and decorating. Smooth off any rough edges with very fine sandpaper. Remove powdered icing with a clean pastry brush. If necessary, repeat with 1 or 2 thin coats of icing.

For square cakes ice 2 opposite sides first. Leave to dry for at least 2 hours before icing the remaining sides. Remove the icing at each side holding the tip of the palette knife parallel with the sides to give sharp corners.

DECORATION ICING

This icing is kneaded together and rolled out like pastry. It is ideal for covering formal rich fruit cakes and novelty all-in-one-cakes. This icing sets firm but not brittle. Cakes do not have to be covered with almond paste or marzipaned first – but this does help to give a smooth base and preserve the cake. Allow the almond paste to dry for up to 1 week before covering with decoration icing. The ingredients make sufficient to cover a 20cm/8in cake.

450g/1 lb icing sugar
one size 2 egg white
1 rounded tbsp glucose syrup
cornflour

Sift the icing sugar. Place the egg white and glucose syrup in a clean grease-free bowl. Add the icing sugar gradually and mix with a wooden spoon. (Or put all but 2 tbsp icing sugar, egg white and glucose syrup in a food processor bowl and work for 30 seconds until mixture is soft and crumbly.) Turn out the mixture and knead in all the icing sugar until the mixture binds together to form a ball. Sprinkle work surface with icing sugar and knead until the mixture is smooth and pliable. If the icing feels too dry and crumbly add a drop more egg white. If the mixture feels a little slack (it should be quite firm) add more icing sugar. Make each batch of icing just before it is required, as it tends to lose its elasticity. Always keep icing wrapped in cling film or in a plastic bag to prevent drying.

To cover cake with decoration icing Put the cake on the cake board. Sprinkle work surface with icing sugar. Roll out icing to a circle 7.5cm/3in larger than the top of the cake. Support the icing over a rolling pin and drape over the cake. Dust hands with cornflour, work in a circular movement rubbing the

icing with the palm of your hand to make the icing thinner, and ease down over the side of the cake, smoothing out folds of icing. This is much easier to do than it sounds. If necessary, trim the edge against the base of the cake.

For a 3-tiered wedding cake Cover a thin cake board with decoration icing. Stand the pillars on this board to take the weight of the remaining tiers. Allow icing to dry for 2–5 days in a cool, dry place before assembling tiers.

Colour and flavour the icing with food colouring and essences (adding a little extra icing sugar if necessary).

Use decoration icing for modelling animals or figures. It can also be cut and rolled, crimped and frilled for flowers and leaves (p.33).

Glucose syrup is a thick clear syrup available from many small chemist shops and from cake decorating suppliers.

GELATINE ICING

This icing can be used in the same way as decoration icing, although it becomes quite brittle as it dries. Use for covering cakes and for cut-out and moulded decorations. The ingredients make sufficient to cover a 20cm/8in cake.

2 tsp gelatine
1 tsp glycerine
1 size 2 egg white
450g/1 lb icing sugar

Measure 2 tbsp of cold water into a small basin and sprinkle in the gelatine. Put the basin in a saucepan of water over a gentle heat. Stir until the gelatine has completely dissolved and the liquid runs clear. Remove from the heat and stir in the glycerine. Sift the icing sugar into a bowl and add the egg white and gelatine mixture. Stir well until firm, then knead with the fingers, adding extra icing sugar if necessary to form a smooth pliable paste. Add colouring and flavouring as desired, with extra icing sugar if necessary. Wrap in a polythene bag.

Gelatine icing is best used straight away but can be stored in a sealed polythene bag for 2–3 days. Place the polythene bag of icing in a basin over hot water to soften slightly and knead again before use. Always keep icing covered in cling film or wrapped in a polythene bag to prevent a crust forming.

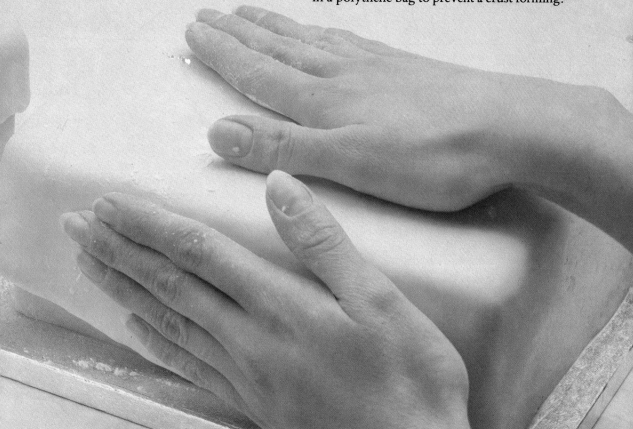

BUTTER ICING

This icing is ideal for novelty birthday cakes and covering sponge and all-in-one cakes. It can be flavoured and coloured to complement the type of cake and pipes easily. Follow the instructions for royal iced piping on p.22. The ingredients make sufficient to cover the top and sides of a 18cm/7in all-in-one cake, or to fill the cake and cover the top only.

100g/4 oz butter or soft tub margarine (chilled)
225g/8 oz icing sugar, sifted

Cream the butter or margarine until soft. Gradually beat in the icing sugar, adding a little hot water and flavouring to give a smooth spreading consistency. To store, place in an airtight container in the refrigerator until required. Leave in a warm place to soften slightly before use.

Flavourings: Vanilla or almond Add a few drops of flavouring to taste. *Peppermint* Add a few drops of flavouring to taste. Colour with green food colouring. *Lemon or orange* Add 1 tsp grated lemon or orange rind and soften the icing with lemon or orange juice. *Chocolate* Add 25g/1 oz melted plain chocolate or dissolve 1–2 tbsp cocoa in a little hot water and beat into the icing. *Coffee* Add 2 tsp instant coffee dissolved in 1 tbsp boiling water.

To cover and fill cake Cut the cake in half or in 3 layers and fill with jam and/or butter icing. Spread the icing around the sides of the cake. Cover the sides of the cake with one of the following: chocolate-flavoured vermicelli, coloured sugar strands, desiccated coconut — toasted under the grill or coloured with 1 or 2 drops of food colouring — crushed cornflakes, toasted flaked almonds, chopped nuts or grated chocolate. Put covering on a large plate or sheet of greaseproof paper, hold the cake on its side and roll carefully onto covering until evenly coated. Place the cake on a serving plate. Spread icing on top of the cake and decorate border with piped butter cream or icing.

RICH BUTTER CREAM

Deliciously rich and smooth this icing does not keep for long – the iced cake can be kept in the refrigerator for up to 3 days. Ideal for whisked sponges, Swiss rolls and all-in-one cakes. The ingredients make sufficient to fill and cover the top of a 20cm/8in cake.

75g/3 oz butter
1 tbsp milk
1 egg yolk
225g/8 oz icing sugar
flavouring as for butter icing

Gently melt the butter in a saucepan over a low heat. It should only just melt and not be too hot. Beat in the milk and egg yolk. Gradually add the icing sugar and beat until the mixture is light and fluffy. To store, place in an airtight container in the refrigerator for up to 3 days.

GLACÉ ICING

Quick and simple to make, glacé icing is useful for icing novelty cakes and can be coloured and flavoured as desired.

225g/8 oz icing sugar
3 tbsp hot water *or* **lemon or orange juice** *or*
    black coffee

Sift the icing sugar into a basin. Add liquid until the mixture thickly coats the back of a spoon.

★*Chocolate glacé icing: dissolve 2 tsp cocoa in the hot water.*

PIPING DESIGNS

BASIC PIPING AND DECORATING

Fine (no. 0) to very thick plain nozzles give a variety of effects. Use a no. 1 or no. 2 for general use.

Line work Use nozzles no. 0, 1, 2 or 3 (pink and orange line). Hold the nozzle just on the cake and press out enough icing to anchor it. Continue pressure and at the same time lift the nozzle so that the line of icing is held about 2.5cm/1in above the cake. Do not pull the thread of icing taut – allow it to fall gently, guiding it along the required line of the pattern, be it straight or curved. When coming to a corner or the end of a line, gently lower the nozzle to touch the surface before starting again. When icing lines against the side of a cake, tilt the cake so that the line falls against the side. Icing which adheres to the nozzles will cause the line to twist so wipe the nozzle clean before each operation. A softer than usual consistency makes working easier – the smaller the hole in the nozzle the softer the consistency needed.

Yellow flower decoration with green leaves Use nozzles no. 1 or 2. Pipe 5 dots in a circle just touching each other. (Make the icing blue for forget-me-nots.)

Each leaf is a dot made by holding the nozzle at an angle to the surface and pulling sideways.

Green line with wavy edge Pipe a straight line first, adding a wavy line or scallops with the same size nozzle or 1 size smaller. As the curves are so small, the nozzle rests on the cake surface all the time.

Pale pink curved lines Pipe a curved line first, following instructions for the straight line. Add dots and scallops on alternate curves. To form dots, place the nozzle at 90° a fraction above the surface and press out a small amount of icing.

Pink ribbon A petal or frill nozzle is cut on the slant and one end is thicker than the other. Guide the thick end of the nozzle along the cake surface, keeping the fine end of the nozzle raised. The frill is made by continuously waving the nozzle back and forth while keeping the thick end of the nozzle firmly on the surface.

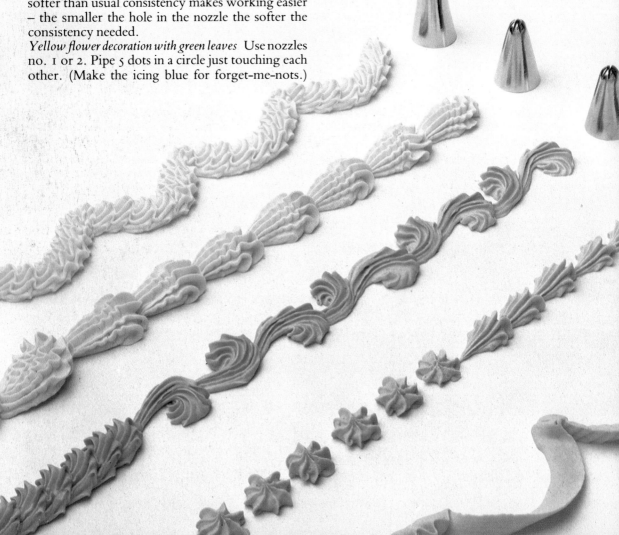

Star nozzles come in many sizes with slightly finer or broader points to give different effects.

Mauve shells Hold the nozzle at 45° just touching the cake. Keep the nozzle still and press the icing out until a rounded head is formed. Release the pressure and gently pull the nozzle away, holding downwards to avoid the tail pointing upwards. Start the next shell 6mm/¼in away and press the icing out until the head forms as before. As the head enlarges it will just meet the tail of the first shell.

Mauve stars Hold nozzle at 90° to the cake, just above the surface. Press once only, keeping nozzle still, release pressure and pull away – the result should be a neat star with a sharp point.

Purple scrolls Hold the nozzle against the cake surface so the icing adheres. Pipe in a circular movement, up, over and down. Release the pressure, drawing the nozzle underneath and away, to produce a thinning tail. The thicker design is achieved by applying pressure continually while moving the nozzle up and around in a whirl. and around in a whirl.

Turquoise border This rather thick border can be used on the side of large cakes. With the star nozzle held against the side of the cake, apply continuous pressure while moving the nozzle up and around in tight whirls, making larger movements as the centre of the curve is reached and reducing the movement again as the curve ends.

BORDERS

All these borders and designs are suitable for royal iced cakes and can be piped in any colour scheme. Make up your own original designs by mixing and matching parts of each border. Practice makes perfect so try your designs out on the edge of a cake tin first.

All these borders are piped with star nozzles and, depending on the number of points to the star, you can achieve varying results.

Stars and stripes Pipe widely spaced large stars around the top edge of the cake. Using a no. 2 nozzle and turquoise icing, pipe a squiggle between each star, piping with a side-to-side motion from the top down over the side of the cake. Using royal blue icing, pipe a curve around each star and a 'V' shape around each squiggle. Repeat this design using turquoise icing around the edge of the cake board. Flood in with soft icing (p.26).

Large shell edging Use a large star nozzle and white icing to pipe the shells around the top edge of the cake. Wiggle the nozzle slightly while piping to give the shells a wavy line. Outline the shells using a no. 2 nozzle and peach-coloured icing.

To decorate the cake board, use a small star nozzle and peach-coloured icing, and pipe a continuous wavy edge 1cm/½in in from the edge of the cake board. Flood in with soft white icing (p.26). Using a no. 2 nozzle and white icing, complete the board decoration by piping a small scallop edge around the outside.

Loop the loop Using a medium star nozzle and white icing, pipe a row of stars onto the top and side of the cake. Using a no. 1 or no. 2 nozzle and pale pink icing, pipe a series of loops from every other star. Pipe all the loops the same length. Allow to dry for 1 hour. Using deep pink icing, pipe a second row of loops onto alternate stars. Loops can be intertwined by piping a loop from the first to the third star, and

from the second to the fourth star, going back to the third and over to the fifth star and so on around the cake. Many arrangements of loops can be achieved by varying length, drop, colour, etc. Individual loops attached to one star give the effect of tassels or tear drops.

To decorate the cake board, use a no. 1 or no. 2 nozzle and pipe a small scallop edge in deep pink icing onto the board. Flood in with soft icing (p.26). Allow to dry for 24 hours. Overpipe with pale pink icing and pipe the elongated dots between each of the deep pink scallops on the board.

Criss-cross border Using a medium star nozzle and white icing, pipe a row of stars around the top edge of the cake. Pipe an equal number of stars below the first row on the side of the cake. Using a no. 3 nozzle, pipe a straight line on top of the cake about 2.5cm/1in from the edge. Overpipe this line with a finer no. 2 nozzle. Using a no. 1 or no. 2 nozzle, pipe diagonal lines, starting from the straight line on top of the cake and bringing the line diagonally over the top of the stars, down and across to the side star, finishing just beneath the adjoining star. Continue piping diagonally in the same direction all the way around the cake. Allow to dry for 1 hour. Pipe lines running diagonally in the opposite direction, crossing the first lines of piping.

To decorate the cake board, pipe a row of small stars around the edge of the board, making sure each star touches the other. Flood in with soft white icing (p.26). Allow to dry for 24 hours. Pipe a row of tiny stars on the side of the cake and another row onto the flooded cake board. Using a no. 1 or no. 2 nozzle, pipe diagonal lines from one star to another. Pipe all the way around the cake and overpipe in the opposite direction.

RUN-OUTS AND BELLS

Run-out numbers, letters, figures and plaques are an attractive way of decorating a cake. They can be piped straight on top of a cake and onto the cake board. If piped on waxed paper and allowed to dry they can be placed in position anywhere on the cake. Trace simple designs from Christmas or birthday cards, children's books or the templates on pp.78–9. Transfer the designs to white card or direct onto the cake.

Use royal icing (coloured as desired) and a no. 1 or no. 2 plain nozzle. Pipe the outline in one continuous line, avoiding breaks which may allow icing to leak out. Soften royal icing with a little egg white or water until it just flows. Fill in the outline with icing using a teaspoon. For small designs it may be easier to pipe icing into the required shape from a greaseproof paper icing bag. Guide the flow into corners with a cocktail stick.

To pipe run-outs direct onto cake Cut out the template and place on the cake. Pipe around outline and remove the template. Or simply outline a design with icing free-hand. Flood in with softened icing.
Separate run-outs These must dry hard so do not add glycerine to the royal icing. Use semi-transparent waxed paper which, when peeled away, gives a smooth base. Place the white card with template outline onto a flat surface such as a tray or board. Secure the waxed paper over the template with a dot of icing. Run-outs are fragile so make extra to allow for breakages. Leave in a warm place for 1–3 days to dry and harden completely. To remove paper, place the run-out over the edge of a table and peel the paper from below a little at a time, moving the run-out around so that a small section at a time is loosened.
Contoured run-outs For the folds of clothing and figures, soften icing just sufficiently with the egg white or water to give the consistency of whipped cream. Place the waxed paper over the template as before. As this icing does not flow, an outline is not required. Simply ice into the shape, applying extra pressure where the design requires extra depth or contour.

With all run-outs, if the design calls for different coloured icing, flood each colour separately. Allow to dry for 2–3 hours before adding the next colour or they may run into each other.

Attach run-outs to the cake with a little royal icing. Fine small details can be overpiped onto run-outs with a fine nozzle.

Bells

To make bells, use white royal icing of a soft piping consistency. Place in a greaseproof paper icing bag and snip off the end, or use a no. 3 piping nozzle. Place the waxed paper over a flat tray or board and secure with a dot of icing. Pipe the icing into small rounded bulbs, keeping the tip of the bag or nozzle buried in the icing as the bulb forms. Gently raise the bag or nozzle to form a pointed bell shape. Allow to dry for 1–2 hours in a warm place until a firm crust forms on the outside of the bell. Carefully lift from the paper and, with a small pointed knife, gently scoop out the soft icing from inside the bell to give a hollow bell shape. Allow to dry completely. Pipe a dot of icing inside the rim of the bell to form the clapper.

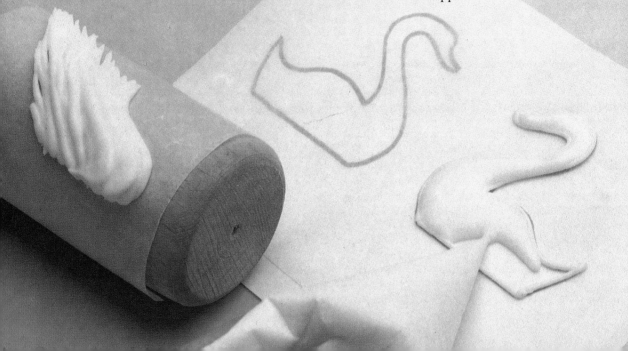

TRELLIS, BASKET AND LACE WORK

Trellis work is often a feature of a design and can either be piped straight onto the top of the cake or onto lightly greased moulds to make open-work baskets or cradles. If you are using a mould, allow the piping enough time to dry (2–3 days) before warming the mould and slipping the piping off. For simple trellis work on top of the cake, use a no. 1 or no. 2 nozzle and pipe parallel lines, spaced 3mm/⅛in apart. Pipe lines similarly spaced in the opposite direction, crossing the first rows.

Cross over the lines at right-angles to make square spaces or diagonally to make diamond spaces. For a fine finish, pipe 2 sets of lines immediately over the base lines, using a finer nozzle – this gives depth to a flat design.

Lace edging

Draw the design onto white paper and mark off parallel lines above and below the design. The lines act as a guide to keep the lace pieces a uniform size. Place waxed paper over the white paper and, using a no. 1 nozzle, pipe the separate pieces of lace between the guide lines. Allow to dry for 24 hours. Carefully remove the lace pieces from the waxed paper and fix to the cake with a little royal icing.

Writing

Using any of the plain nozzles – no. 1, 2 or 3 – and keeping the nozzle on the cake while icing, all types of writing style can be achieved. A fancy style of capital letter gives a lift to plain writing. Birthday and Christmas cards often have styles which can be copied. A book on calligraphy from the local library is worth perusing.

If you prefer, write the name or greeting onto greaseproof paper first, place over the dried cake icing and prick out using a pin or needle.

Random lace

This effect can be achieved by using either a no. 1 or no. 2 nozzle. Pipe with the nozzle resting on the surface of the cake and continuously wriggle the nozzle around in tight random swirls. Move sideways and downwards – not upwards. This effect can be put to good use in hiding a poorly finished surface!

Basket work

Use royal or butter icing for basket work. You will need 2 icing nozzles for basket work – a basket nozzle with a serrated edge (or a plain ribbon nozzle) and a plain nozzle, no. 3 or no. 2. Always start and finish the work at the back of the cake or box.

Start the horizontal wickerwork with the basket nozzle. Pipe 2.5cm/1in lengths of icing, the width of the nozzle apart, down the side of the cake. Using the plain nozzle, pipe a vertical length of cane from the top of the cake to the bottom, piping just over the right edge of the wickerwork. Change to a basket nozzle and pipe wickerwork strips in the open spaces. Start 1cm/½in before the vertical cane, work over the cane and finish 1cm/½in the other side, making each length 2.5cm/1in as before.

Pipe another vertical cane over the ends of this extended wickerwork. Check that the end of the basket nozzle is clean each time. Pipe to the side of the cane that adjoins the first wickerwork row and pipe another row of wickerwork, carrying it over the second cane. The basket shape is now apparent. Continue in a similar fashion all round the cake.

If a lid is required, use a thin silver board of a suitable size and pipe icing onto the white surface of the board. Balance the lid on a basin while piping. Using a large star nozzle, finish the basket and lid with an edging of scrolls.

FLOWERS AND FRILLS

PIPING ROSES, FLOWERS AND LEAVES

For all flowers, unless you are piping straight onto the cake, use a cork placed on a skewer or a flower icing nail with 2.5cm/1in squares of non-stick or waxed papers.

Making flowers, particularly roses, is an art worth achieving, although it needs practice and perseverence. Nozzles vary from the very tiny to the large petal, curved and straight. Practice first with a medium straight nozzle. This is a nozzle with a flat slanted cut, one point thicker than the other. Place a wine-bottle cork on a skewer or buy a flower nail. (1) Holding the skewer in your left hand and the icing bag in your right hand, put a blob of icing on the cork. (2) Press a 2.5cm/1in square piece of waxed or non-stick paper to the icing. (3) Stab the thick point of the nozzle onto the paper, making a dent into the icing below. Pipe a cone of coiled ribbon to form a standing bud by bringing the ribbon towards yourself and at the same time slowly revolve the cork anti-clockwise. When a continuous coil has formed turn the nozzle downwards to end. (4) For the first petal place the thick point of the nozzle close to the bud, tilt the nozzle to the right, then swivel it on its point over to the left. In this way the icing will stand in a half circle. Pipe 3 petals to form the rose. Each petal should start with the point of the nozzle placed at the end of the previous petal. (5) Slip off the paper and rose and put on a tray in a warm place to dry for 1 day. (6) Peel away paper and fix the rose to the cake with a blob of icing. Roses can be stored for future use. Do not, however, seal into polythene boxes. Always use a cardboard box.

Pansy, primrose, narcissus, apple blossom and Christmas roses Colour the icing to suit the flower. These petals all lie flat on the paper. Use a medium, flat petal nozzle. Put the thick point to the centre. Radiate the nozzle just far enough to make 1 rounded petal, release pressure and draw off the nozzle to the centre. As the nozzle radiates, move it outwards just a little if the petal is pointed as for the narcissus. Move the nozzle in and out twice for heart-shaped primrose petals – these movements are slight and take practice. Pipe 5 petals (6 for narcissus) to make 1 flower. Pipe the centres with a no. 1 nozzle – yellow dots for apple blossom and Christmas roses, 1 yellow dot for the pansy, a green dot for the primrose and a yellow or orange circle for the narcissus.

Violet Use a small petal nozzle and follow the technique illustrated opposite.

Sweet pea Use a medium petal nozzle and follow the technique illustrated opposite.

Daisy flower Hold a straight petal nozzle vertical to the paper with the opening just a fraction above and press once. This gives a petal pointed at both ends the same shape as the nozzle opening. Pipe as many petals as are required, radiating from the centre. Pipe a large dot over the centre.

Simple flowers can be made with a no. 1 or no. 2 plain nozzle or simply snip a paper icing bag to make a small hole. These flowers can be piped straight onto the cake, although some are best piped onto waxed paper.

Forget-me-nots Pipe 5 blue dots all touching in a circle, with 1 yellow dot in the middle.

Simple daisies Pipe tear drops radiating from a yellow dot.

Other flowers can be made with heart-shaped dots. Pipe 2 tear drops together to make 1 heart-

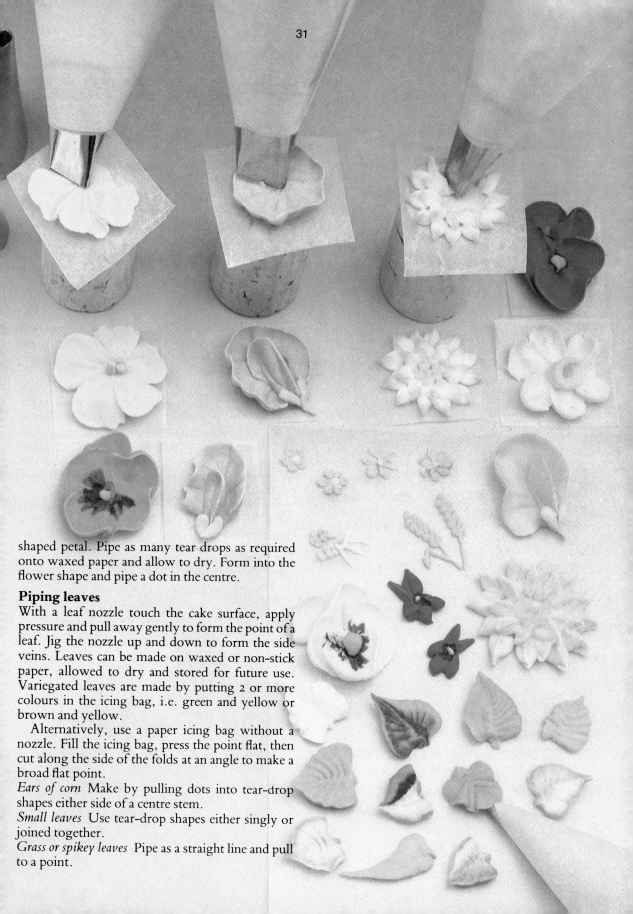

shaped petal. Pipe as many tear drops as required onto waxed paper and allow to dry. Form into the flower shape and pipe a dot in the centre.

Piping leaves

With a leaf nozzle touch the cake surface, apply pressure and pull away gently to form the point of a leaf. Jig the nozzle up and down to form the side veins. Leaves can be made on waxed or non-stick paper, allowed to dry and stored for future use. Variegated leaves are made by putting 2 or more colours in the icing bag, i.e. green and yellow or brown and yellow.

Alternatively, use a paper icing bag without a nozzle. Fill the icing bag, press the point flat, then cut along the side of the folds at an angle to make a broad flat point.

Ears of corn Make by pulling dots into tear-drop shapes either side of a centre stem.

Small leaves Use tear-drop shapes either singly or joined together.

Grass or spikey leaves Pipe as a straight line and pull to a point.

MODELLING ROSES, FLOWERS AND LEAVES

Modelling paste is firm enough to roll out very thinly, dries quickly and keeps its shape. It is ideal for modelling delicate roses.

1 rounded tsp gelatine
1 rounded tsp white fat
5 tsp cold water
225g/8 oz icing sugar

Place the gelatine, fat and water in a small saucepan. Heat gently until the fat and gelatine has dissolved and the liquid is clear. Gradually stir in the icing sugar until the mixture forms a firm ball. Turn out and knead in the remaining icing sugar – you may need a little more – until the paste is firm but pliable. Always keep the paste covered in a poly-thene bag or cling film to prevent drying.

There are many flower, petal and leaf cutters available to make a wide range of flowers. Flowers can be modelled in decoration or gelatine icing as well as modelling paste, and in some instances almond paste or marzipan can be used.

★ *Decorations made with this modelling paste will keep for an indefinite period if kept dry.*

Modelling a rose

Very lightly grease the work surface, your hands and the rolling pin with white fat. Take a small piece of modelling paste and form into a cone shape. Roll out a small ball of paste into a strip and wind the strip around the top of the cone, covering the tip completely so that it looks like the tightly curled centre of a rose. Roll out small balls of paste into petal shapes, flattening the edges between your finger and thumb. Brush the base of each petal very lightly with egg white and press in turn onto the rose, overlapping petals until the rose is the required size.

The rose will look more realistic if the edge of each petal is rolled back slightly. You may find it easier to shape each petal over a large wooden bead or any round object to achieve the same effect.

Model a rosebud by taking a small cone of icing and wrapping 1 or 2 petals tightly around the cone.

Green sepals Use green-coloured paste and model 5 oval sepals, tipping each one with egg white. Push the sepals onto the top of a small green ball of paste, lightly brush with egg white and secure to the underside of the finished rose. With a large rose, curl away the sepals – with a bud the sepal stays on the petals. Model the rose stem by rolling a little green paste into a long thin strip and attach the strip to the rose sepal.

Rose leaves Pick and clean a rose leaf from the garden and very lightly grease the underside of the leaf. Press green-coloured paste onto the underside of the leaf and carefully break the paste away from the edges of the leaf to create a jagged effect. Carefully pull the paste away from the leaf and the veins will appear on the paste. Leave to dry curved over crumpled kitchen paper. If there are no real rose leaves available, simply cut out oval leaf shapes and mark the veins with the back of a knife, or use a flower cutter.

Flowers and leaves

Christmas roses Using a small round cutter or the broad end of a piping nozzle, cut out the petals. Place each petal in the palm of your hand and press with a round-handled knife to curve the petal. Carefully press one end to a slight point. Allow the petals to dry overnight. Pipe large dots of yellow royal icing onto waxed or silicone paper or direct onto the cake, and arrange 5 petals around and into each dot. Lightly brush green strokes of food colouring on each petal and pipe tiny yellow dots of royal icing around the centre. Allow to dry for at least 24 hours until firm.

Primroses Shape a small cone of yellow almond paste over the end of a paint brush. With a cocktail stick make 5 dents around the top edge. Using a small pair of scissors, make cuts between the dents to form 5 petals. Press each petal between your fingers to flatten and open out, and gently curve the corners.

Primrose leaves Roll green icing or paste into small sausages, flatten with a rolling pin and use the back of a knife to mark in the veins.

Carnations Roll and cut out 5cm/2in circles from the decoration icing or modelling paste. Roll the edge of each circle with a cocktail stick. Brush the centres with a little egg white and fold in half. Repeat and fold in half again. Leave to dry overnight on crumpled cling film before placing on the cake.

Narcissus or daffodil Model 6 petal shapes for each flower, lightly marking a line down the centre of each petal with the back of a knife and pointing the ends slightly.

To make a trumpet, take a small ball of paste or icing and push in a plain nozzle to make a wide hole. Roll the edge with a cocktail stick to flute the trumpet. Stand the trumpet flute-side down and, with a dot of egg white, overlap each petal around the trumpet base. Allow to dry overnight before placing on the cake.

MODELLING ANIMALS AND FIGURES

Animals and figures can be modelled in decoration or gelatine icing as well as modelling paste, and in some instances almond paste or marzipan can be used. Roll out the icing or paste on a work surface well dusted with cornflour.

Choir boys Roll red paste or icing into a small cone shape to make the body. For the ruffle, either pipe around the body with white royal icing, using a ribbon or frill nozzle, or cut out a circle of decoration icing, frill with a cocktail stick and place on top of the body. To make the hands, roll a little pink icing or paste into small balls, flatten and fold in half, and press onto the body. Roll a larger ball for the head and paint on the features with a little food colouring.

Robin and lantern Shape and paint with food colouring as shown.

Mr and Mrs Use decoration or gelatine icing, almond paste or marzipan to make these figures. The basic shapes can be painted to create any characters you like. Allow the figures to dry on greaseproof paper for 24 hours or until firm, before painting with food colouring. Paint the back of each

figure, lay face down on cotton wool to dry, turn over and paint the front. Allow to dry completely before placing on the cake. If necessary, secure the figures with a little royal or butter icing, or with cocktail sticks.

Holly Thinly roll out the green paste or icing and cut out the shapes using a holly leaf cutter. Or cut out small oblong shapes, mark a line down the centre with the back of a knife and use a teaspoon to bite out the shape of the holly. Roll a little red icing into berries.

MAKING FRILLS, FLOUNCES AND FLOWERS

There is no need to do any piping on a celebration cake if you use decoration icing. You can add frills around the base of the cake, flounces around the sides and decorate with pretty flowers using one simple method of rolling and frilling. Before beginning to ice any cake read these instructions in conjunction with the design you are following. Use the basic decoration icing (p.18). Gelatine icing can also be used but it is not quite so pliable to work with and becomes more brittle when dry.

Dust the work surface, your hands and the rolling pin, cutters or cocktail stick with cornflour. Roll out small pieces of icing according to the size of the cake and the design. Only roll 1 piece of icing at a time, keeping the remainder well covered with cling film or wrapped in a polythene bag.

To make side flounces Roll out and trim icing to a strip about 5–7.5 × 1cm/2–3 × ½in or as required. Using your index finger, roll a cocktail stick firmly across the strip to frill the edge. The icing will curve away from you, so ease the icing back into line, lifting the frills with the cocktail stick. Move the flounce slightly to make sure it does not stick to the work surface.

To make base frills Frills for the base of a cake need to be wider, with the straight flat edge resting against the side of the cake and curving down onto the board. Roll out and trim icing into strips about 20 × 2.5cm/8 × 1in or as required. With the back of a knife mark a line 6mm/¼in in from the long edge. Roll with a cocktail stick up to this line and frill using the same method as for the flounces.

To attach frills and flounces to cake Place each frill or flounce on the cake as it is made or the icing will harden and crumble. Using an artist's paint brush, brush the cake with a very little water, either along the base for a frill, or in gentle curves about halfway up the side of the cake as shown. Carefully lift and curve the icing against the side of the cake and press lightly to secure. Roll out the next frill or flounce and place on the cake, lightly pressing the strips together at the joins to smooth out the seams. If

liked, roll a dressmaker's tracing wheel along the straight edge to give a stitched effect.

To make flowers Use a small 1cm/½in fluted or plain cutter for small flowers and a 2.5cm/1in round cutter for larger flowers. Roll and cut out the icing and flute the flowers all the way round using a cocktail stick. Make a tiny hole in the centre if you wish to place fabric flowers through the icing flowers as shown. Allow to dry overnight on a tray lined with greaseproof paper.

To attach the flowers to the side of the cake, roll tiny pieces of icing trimmings into small balls, brush the centre of the back of the flowers with a dot of egg white and press a ball of icing onto each flower. (If you are using fabric flowers, push the stalk through the hole and push the icing ball onto the stalk.) Brush the ball of icing with a dot of egg white and press onto the cake or secure the flowers with a dot of royal icing.

To make shells Roll out a little icing and cut out a circle using a 5–6.5cm/2–2½in fluted pastry cutter. Using the handle of an artist's paint brush, press and roll lightly as shown. To thread with ribbon, make tiny holes with the end of the paint brush at the top of each frill. Curve the shell gently and leave to dry against a strip of greaseproof paper in a wine glass for at least 2 days. When dry, thread carefully with narrow ribbon.

Always make extra flowers or shells to allow for breakages.

To paint edges of flowers or frills Allow the icing to dry for 24 hours or the colouring will run. Use an artist's fine paint brush, dip lightly into food colouring and just touch the edges of the icing.

ENGAGEMENT AND VALENTINE CAKES

FOR EVER AND ALWAYS

**25cm/10in round or horseshoe-shaped rich
   fruit cake (pp.8–9)**
almond paste (pp.14–15)
royal icing (p.16)
12in round or horseshoe-shaped cake board
food colourings: mauve and pink
nozzles: no. 1, 2 and 3 plain
5 carnations (p.33)
6 white frilled flowers (p.37)
a few sprigs of green fern

To cut a horseshoe-shaped cake, bake in a round tin
of the required size. Using a paper pattern, cut out a
central circle between 7.5cm/3in and 10cm/4in in
diameter, depending on the size of the cake. Place
the pattern over the cake, carefully cut the cake
using a sharp knife and cut a wedge-shaped piece
from the top (see diagram).

Cover the cake with almond paste and place on
the board. Colour the icing a pale mauve.

To flat ice cake Ice the outside edge of the cake, then
flat ice the inside curve using a palette knife to
sweep the icing smooth. Allow to dry and flat ice
the 2 straight ends. Allow to dry before flat icing
the top. Repeat with a second thin coat. Allow to
dry for 24 hours.

To decorate border Using white royal icing and a
no. 3 nozzle, pipe a row of dots around the top and
bottom edges of the cake, on the side of the cake
and on the cake board; pipe another dot between
every second and third dot and another dot
between these 2 to give a lace effect.

Using a no. 2 nozzle, pipe the names onto the
cake. Change to a no. 1 nozzle and overpipe the
names. Colour the remaining icing a deep mauve
and pipe tiny hearts around the sides of the cake by
piping 2 pear-shaped dots together as shown.

Secure the carnations and white flowers to the
cake with a dot of icing and arrange green fern
between the flowers.

VALENTINE CAKE

23cm/9in heart-shaped rich fruit cake (pp.8–9)
almond paste (pp.14–15)
royal icing (p.16)
12in heart-shaped cake board
nozzles: no. 1 and 2 plain, medium star
food colourings: pink, blue, yellow
**   and burgundy**

Cover the cake with almond paste and place on the board. Flat ice the top and sides and allow to dry for 24 hours. If necessary, apply a second thin coat. Allow to dry for 48 hours before applying the run-out heart.

Run-out heart Using a no. 2 nozzle and royal icing, pipe a smaller heart outline on top of the cake. Soften a little pink icing with egg white or water until it just flows and flood into the heart outline. Allow to dry for 48 hours.

To decorate cake board Using a no. 2 nozzle and pink icing, pipe a scalloped outline 1cm/½in in from the edge of the cake board. Flood in with softened pink icing as above. Allow to dry for 48 hours. Using a no. 1 nozzle and burgundy icing, repeat the scallop outline on top of the run-out and pipe pips around the edge of the run-out. Pipe small burgundy scallops at the base of the cake. Pipe a matching decoration onto the heart on top of the cake.

To decorate border Using a medium star nozzle and burgundy icing, pipe 2 rows of stars. Outline the sides of the stars using a no. 2 nozzle with pink icing.

To decorate sides Using a no. 1 nozzle, pipe 5 small dots around a centre dot for each flower. Pipe 3 flowers, 1 pink, 1 yellow and 1 blue, and pipe the ribbon in pink. With a no. 1 nozzle and burgundy icing, make the hearts by piping 2 pear-shaped dots close together.

★ *This also serves as an engagement cake. To complete the decoration, use a no. 1 nozzle with blue icing and write the names and 'congratulations' on top of the heart.*

WEDDING CAKES

To assemble a wedding cake place 4 pillars between each tier. Choose round or square pillars according to the cake.

A cake stand and knife can usually be hired from confectioners and are plastic, silver-plated or mirrored. Assemble the cake an hour or so before the reception: it is safer not to leave the cake standing for too long. With extra large cakes or should the icing be too soft to hold the tiers, put a thin silver board on top of the bottom tier to take the pillars. If you wish, the board can be iced over.

When the bride and groom cut the cake, they should push the tip of the knife into the top of the bottom tier and then pull the knife down. The caterers will then dismantle the cake and take away the bottom tier to finish cutting it.

It is usual for the bottom tier to be eaten at the reception, the middle tier to be cut up to send to absent friends and relations, and the top tier to be stored for a future occasion – for example, a wedding anniversary or the birth of the first child.

PEACHES AND CREAM

two square rich fruit cakes: 25cm/10in and
  18cm/7in (pp.8–9)
almond paste (pp.14–15)
royal icing (p.16)
two square gold cake boards: 14in and 10in
food colourings: yellow, pink, orange and
  brown
nozzles: no. 1 and 2 plain, shell or star and
  forget-me-not
4 gold cake pillars
decoration for top: fresh or fabric flower
  arrangement

Cover the cakes with almond paste and place on the boards. Colour the royal icing cream by using yellow colouring with a drop of pink, and mix well. Flat ice the tops and sides of the cakes. Allow to dry for 24 hours and put on a second thin coat. Allow to dry for 24 hours.

To decorate border Using a shell or star nozzle, pipe a shell border with cream-coloured royal icing.
Flower border Tint the royal icing in 4 different tones of peach colour. Mix yellow, orange and pink colours into the royal icing to get a good peach colour. Split the icing into 4 small basins. Tint each batch a different tone by adding white icing or more colouring as necessary. Using the deepest peach tone and the forget-me-not nozzle, pipe flowers onto the cake boards and pipe just a few on the sides of the cakes. Change the colour tone and pipe at random, filling in the spaces so that the boards and lower sides are completely covered. Cut the tip of a greaseproof paper icing bag into a small leaf shape. Fill the bag with brown-coloured royal icing and pipe leaves amongst the flowers.

Complete the decoration by outlining the border with peach-coloured royal icing using a no. 1 or no. 2 nozzle. Assemble the cake and place a fresh or fabric flower arrangement on top.
★ *To make a thick cake stand, place 3 cake boards on top of each other and cover with a wide gold cake band.*

SPRINGTIME

Primroses are ideal for a Spring wedding, but you can make these flowers in any colour to suit any season.

**three square rich fruit cakes: 25cm/10in,
    20cm/8in and 15cm/6in (pp.8–9)
almond paste (pp.14–15)
royal icing (p.16)
three square cake boards: 12in, 10in and 8in
food colourings: yellow and green
nozzles: no. 1 plain, small and medium star
66 yellow primroses (p.30)
110 yellow lace pieces (p.28)
8 white cake pillars
decoration for top**

Cover the cakes with almond paste and place on the boards. Flat ice the tops and sides of the cakes and allow to dry for 24 hours. Cover with a second thin coat of icing and allow to dry for 24 hours.

To decorate borders (p.24) Using a star nozzle and white royal icing, pipe a border along the top edges as shown. Using the same nozzle, pipe the bottom borders with standing shells. Using a no. 1 nozzle and pale green icing, outline the borders on the top and sides of each cake and on the cake boards.

To decorate top Cut 3 squares of paper as templates 6.5cm/2½in smaller than each cake and place on the cakes. Using yellow royal icing and a small star nozzle, pipe a square of small shells around the outside of each template, take the paper away and, while the shells are still soft, insert the yellow lace pieces so that they stand upright. Using yellow royal icing of a slightly softer consistency and a no. 1 nozzle, pipe a random lace design (p.29) between the squares and the borders.

Secure the primroses onto the cakes with a little royal icing. Put pale green icing in a greaseproof paper icing bag and snip the end into a leaf shape (p.31). Pipe leaves between the primroses. Using yellow icing and a no. 1 nozzle, pipe a curved line of single dots between the primroses. Assemble the cakes, using 4 pillars between each tier, and add the decoration for the top.

RED ROSES FOR THE BRIDE

Make this stunning yet simple cake with ribbons to match the bride's bouquet or the bridesmaids' dresses.

25cm/10in round rich fruit cake (pp.8–9)
almond paste (optional) (pp.14–15)
1.5kg/3 lb decoration icing (p.18)
12in round cake board
food colouring: red
32 white decoration icing flowers
32 red fabric flowers
1m/1yd red velvet ribbon, 6mm/¼in wide
15 × 2.5cm/6 × 1in red ribbon
decoration for top: a silver-coloured heart shape

Cover the cake with almond paste (if using). Place the cake on the board and cover with 900g/2 lb of the decoration icing.

Flowers and frills (p.36) Make up a further 450g/1 lb of decoration icing and cut in half. Cut 1 piece into 6 and wrap the rest of the icing in cling film. Roll out each piece to an oblong 20 × 2.5cm/8 × 1in. Mark a line 6mm/¼in in from one long side and roll with a cocktail stick to frill. Brush the base of the cake with a little water and press the frill against the cake. Repeat to completely cover the base of the cake. To make flowers, roll and cut out the remaining icing using a 2.5cm/1in cutter. Flute with a cocktail stick. Make a tiny hole in the centre of each flower. Allow to dry for 24 hours. Brush the edges lightly with a little red food colouring. Push the fabric flower stalks through the hole into the icing flowers and snip off the ends. Brush the centre of the back of the icing flowers with a dot of egg white. Press a tiny ball of icing onto each stalk. Brush each ball of icing with a dot of egg white and press onto the cake, or secure the flowers with a dot of royal icing.

Wrap the red velvet ribbon around the base of the cake and secure with a little icing. To make the decoration for the top of the cake, knead the icing trimmings and form into a small dome about 4cm/1½in high and 5cm/2in wide. Place the silver heart on top of the dome, press 5 flowers around the top and wrap the wide red ribbon around the base.

FRILLS AND FLOUNCES FOR A WEDDING

This design looks pretty in any colour and can be used for square or round cakes up to 3 tiers high.

Cover the base tier with decoration icing at least 2 weeks before the wedding.

two square rich fruit cakes: 25cm/10in and 20cm/8in (pp.8–9)
almond paste (optional) (pp.14–15)
1.8kg/4 lb decoration icing (p.18)
royal icing (p.16)
two square cake boards: 12in and 10in
food colourings: yellow, orange and apricot
nozzle: no. 2 plain
4 cake pillars
decoration for top: fabric flower arrangement plus a small bunch of flowers to place between the pillars

Cover the cakes with almond paste (if using) and place on the boards. Make 1kg/2 lb of decoration icing and cover the larger cake. Make up the rest of the decoration icing, cut in half and use only 450g/1 lb to cover the small cake.

To decorate sides Divide the sides of each cake into 3 equal sections, marking each section with the point of a cocktail stick. Tint the remaining decoration icing with a little yellow food colouring to give a very pale yellow colour. Cut in half and tint one half with orange colouring. Remember that the

colours will be paler when the icing is rolled out thinly. Tint the royal icing a slightly deeper shade with apricot colouring. Cover all the icings with cling film.

To make frills Using the pale orange decoration icing for the small cake, roll a tiny piece of icing the size of half a walnut into a sausage shape. Roll out thinly and trim to an oblong 6.5 × 1cm/2½ × ½in. Using a cocktail stick, roll the icing to frill (p.36). Using an artist's paint brush, very lightly brush a little cold water in a curved line between the marks, about half way up the side of the cake. Carefully lift each frill and curve onto the side of the cake. Trim to fit the curve. Repeat on the other sides of the cake. Slightly curve each frill under at the joins. Smooth the joins together.

Using the same pale apricot icing for the larger cake, roll out slightly bigger pieces of icing to oblongs 9cm/3½in long and repeat the frills as for the small cake. Using yellow decoration icing, repeat the rolling and frilling as before. Place the frills about 1cm/½in above the orange frills. If you wish, use a dressmaker's tracing wheel and run along the fixed edge of the frills to decorate.

To pipe border and decoration Using a no. 2 plain nozzle and apricot royal icing, pipe a row of large dots around the base of both cakes. Pipe another 2 dots against every second and third dot and 1 dot

against these 2 dots to form a lace edging. Pipe tiny dots on the sides of the cakes between every third and fourth dot. Tilt each cake slightly and pipe a curved line on top of each frill, piping a bow at each point. Pipe a curved row of 5 dots, finishing with 2 elongated dots at each end between the bows.

Assemble the cakes placing a small bunch of flowers between the pillars and a fabric flower decoration on the top tier.

A CLASSIC WEDDING CAKE

**three round rich fruit cakes: 25cm/10in,
20cm/8in and 15cm/6in (pp.8–9)**
almond paste (pp.14–15)
royal icing (p.16)
three round cake boards: 13in, 11in and 9in
**nozzles: no. 1 and 2 plain, small and medium
star**
15 large, 15 medium and 12 small roses (p.30)
24 white bells (p.26)
**3m/3yd silver-paper cake board edging,
1cm/½in wide**
9 round cake pillars
**decoration for top: fresh or fabric flower
arrangement**

Cover the cakes with almond paste and place on the
boards. Flat ice the tops and sides, allow to dry and
cover with a second thin coat of royal icing. Allow
to dry for 24 hours.

To decorate boards Using a small star nozzle, pipe a
row of stars close to the edge of each board, making
sure the stars touch each other. Soften some of the
white royal icing with egg white or water until it
just flows. Flood onto the boards, prick out any air
bubbles that form and leave to dry for 24 hours.

To decorate borders Cut 3 circles of paper 5cm/2in
smaller than each cake and place on the centre top of
each cake as a template. Using a no. 2 nozzle, pipe a
circular line around the outside of each template.
Remove the templates. Using a no. 1 nozzle, pipe a
decorative edging (p.25) inside each circle. Pipe stars
and a criss-cross border around the top of each cake
(p.25). The diagonal lines should start at the edge of
the piped circle.

To decorate sides Divide the side of each cake into
4 equal sections, marking with a dot of icing. Place
3 roses in a slightly curving line between each
section, securing each rose with a little icing. Using
a no. 2 plain nozzle, pipe a bow at the point of each
section and while the icing is still soft attach the
bells.

Pipe a curved line between the bows and the
roses.

With dots of icing secure the silver-paper edging
around the cake boards. Assemble the cakes, using
4 pillars between each tier, and place the flower
arrangement on top.

ROSES ALL THE WAY

three round rich fruit cakes: 25cm/10in,
  20cm/8in and 15cm/6in (pp.8–9)
almond paste (p.14–15)
royal icing (p.16)
three round cake boards: 13in, 8in and 6in
food colourings: pink, red, green and yellow
nozzles: no. 1 and 2 plain and star
50 large pale pink roses (p.30)
30 medium pink roses (p.30)
20 small deep pink roses (p.30)
30 very pale pink blossoms (p.30)
waxed or non-stick paper

Cover the cakes with almond paste and place on the
boards. Flat ice the tops and sides – to ice the sides
of the 20cm/8in and 15cm/6in cakes, stand the cakes
on waxed or non-stick paper and ice the sides down
over the cake boards onto the paper. Allow to dry
for 24 hours and cover with a second thin coat of
royal icing. Allow at least 7 days to dry and harden.

To decorate large board Using a no. 1 or no. 2 nozzle,
pipe a line on the outer edge of the cake board.
Soften about 8 tbsp of royal icing with egg white or
water until it just flows. Flood the cake board, prick
out any air bubbles and leave to dry for 24 hours.
To decorate borders Using a star nozzle, pipe a white
shell border around the top of each cake. Outline
the shells using a no. 1 nozzle and pink royal icing.
To assemble cake Cut the waxed or non-stick paper
under the 20cm/8in and 15cm/6in cakes to the exact
size of the cake boards. Keep the paper under the
boards to protect the icing on top of the cake
beneath.

Place the cakes centrally one on top of the other.
Using a medium star nozzle and white royal icing,
pipe a shell border around the base of each cake to
cover the joins and around the edge of the board on
the bottom tier. Make a dome of very thick royal
icing on the top tier and cover with roses. Secure
the roses and blossoms with a little icing, arranging
them in 2 spirals, back and front, down over the 3
tiers. Put pale green icing in a greaseproof paper
icing bag and snip the end into a leaf shape (p.31).
Pipe leaves between the roses.

CHRISTENING CAKES

A CHRISTENING CRADLE

18cm/7in rich fruit cake (p.8–9)
   baked in a greased and lined 1kg/2 lb loaf
   tin for 3½–4 hours
almond paste
decoration icing (p.18)
10in square cake board
food colouring: pink
1 small plastic baby doll
cocktail stick
1m/1 yd narrow blue ribbon
30 × 15cm/12 × 6in piece white net
2 white pipe cleaners

Cover the cake with almond paste. Place the cake on the board. Reserve half the decoration icing and wrap tightly in cling film or a polythene bag. Dust work surface with cornflour. Roll remaining icing to a rectangle 30 × 23cm/12 × 9in and place over the cake. Dust hands with cornflour and carefully ease icing down over the sides of the cake, taking fullness out of the corners and onto the sides. Trim edges. Mix any trimmings with remaining icing.
To decorate cake Colour half of the remaining icing a deep pink. Roll 3 small pieces about the size of a walnut into sausage shapes. Cover with cling film. Dust work surface with cornflour and roll 1 piece at a time into a strip about 2.5cm/1in wide × 15cm/6in long. Roll with a cocktail stick to frill (p.36). Brush a little water around the base of the cake. Press the straight edge of the frill against the cake, allowing it to curve down onto the board. Lift the curves of the frill slightly with the cocktail stick. Repeat with remaining 2 pieces to cover base with frill. Roll out a small pillow about 5 × 2.5cm/2 × 1in and place on top of the cake. Surround with a deep pink frill 1cm/½in wide. Place the baby doll on the cake.

   Knead remaining deep pink icing into white icing to give a pale pink colour. (Add colour if necessary.) Roll out 3 more strips of icing to only 1cm/½in wide and repeat frilling. Brush the cake with water and press the frill onto the side of the cake to just overlap deep pink frill. Roll remaining pale pink icing to an oblong 18 × 14cm/7in × 5½in. Frill 3 sides with a cocktail stick, drape over the doll and cake and fold back top unfrilled edge. Use basket, star and plain icing nozzles and press points lightly into icing to make a decorative pattern. Wrap the blue ribbon around the top of the pink frill and tie in a small bow. Tie another small bow and place at the top of the blanket. Twist the ends of the pipe cleaners together. Push one end into the

frill at the head of the cradle. Bend the other end over the cake. Drape the net over the pipe cleaner and tie the remaining ribbon into a bow over the end.

LITTLE BOY BLUE

20cm/8in square rich fruit cake (pp.8–9)
almond paste (pp.14–15)
royal icing (p.16)
11in square cake board
10cm/4in white ribbon
food colourings: blue and orange
nozzles: no. 1 and 2 plain, medium star
small plastic baby doll
run–out swan (p.26)

Cover the cake with almond paste and place on the board. Flat ice top and sides with pale blue royal icing. Allow to dry.
To decorate board Divide each side of the cake board into 5 equal sections. Mark each with a small dot of icing 1cm/½in from the edge of the cake. Use a no. 2 plain nozzle and pipe a curved line with blue icing between each dot to form the scallop edge. Put 4 tbsp of blue icing into a small bowl and soften with a little egg white or water until it just flows. Put icing into greaseproof paper icing bag and snip off the end. Pipe into the centre of each scallop allowing the icing to flow out to the outline. Allow to dry for 24 hours.
Swan Follow directions for run-outs and contour run-out for wings (p.26). Trace off the template on p.79. You will need 2 swan bodies (left and right), 2 wings (left and right) and a base, plus extra to allow for breakages. When the run-outs are completely dry and hard, paint on the beak and eyes with food colouring. Sandwich the bodies together with a little icing and put a good-sized blob of icing onto the base. Stand the body on the base with the wings each side curving inwards. When dry and firm place a piece of folded ribbon inside the wings and sit the baby doll on the ribbon. With a short piece of thread make the reins – attaching them to the baby's hands and swan with dots of icing.
To decorate borders With white icing and a no. 1 plain nozzle pipe lace edging around run-out on the cake board. With a medium star nozzle, pipe stars around the top edge of the cake. With blue icing and either a no. 1 or no. 2 plain nozzle overpipe the stars with circular loops. Outline stars on the inside edge with a curved line.
To decorate sides Pipe blue forget-me-not flowers (p.30). Join with dots and bows in white using a no. 1 nozzle.

CRINOLINE LADIES

**rich fruit cake mixture sufficient for a
15cm/6in round cake (p.8–9)
or all–in–one cake (p.10)**
almond paste (optional) (p.14–15)
royal icing (p.16) or butter icing (p.20)
round cake board, 2in larger than basin
**food colourings: pink, yellow, violet and
green**
nozzles: no. 1 and 2 plain, medium frill
plastic doll
**a few small roses in different colours for
bouquet, dress and hat**
modelling paste (p.32)

Place the cake upside down on the board and cover with almond paste (if using). Remove the plastic doll's legs, or cut a hole in the cake, wrap the doll in cling film and push through the cake. China or plaster busts are available from cake decorating suppliers and from craft shops. Fix the doll on top with extra almond paste padded around the base of the figure to make the 'skirt' flow from the waist. (Use butter icing in the same way.)

To decorate dress With a round-ended knife spread cream-coloured icing – yellow and a little pink well mixed into the royal icing gives a cream colour – onto the front portion of the skirt, smoothing the icing downwards. The lines left by the knife give the appearance of folds. Using the frill nozzle (p.36) and cream-coloured icing, pipe 2 layers of frills at the base of the skirt. Build up the frills from the base following the illustrated design or make up your own dress style. Before the icing dries, place a few roses on the skirt and arrange a few more to make the bouquet. Pipe tiny leaves amongst the flowers (p.31).

Roll out the modelling paste onto a greased surface, cut out a circle with a pastry cutter and model by hand into the shape of a hat. To keep the brim curved, place over crumpled kitchen paper and leave to dry for 24 hours. Put the hat on the doll's head and secure with a dot of icing. Arrange roses on the hat and secure with a dot of icing.

★ *For the all-in-one cake bake in a 900ml/ 1½ pint basin for 1 hour – 1 hour 15 minutes. Or, for smaller cakes, divide the mixture between a 600ml/ 1 pint basin (bake for 55 minutes–1 hour) and a 300ml/½ pint basin (bake for 40 minutes). Bake the rich fruit cake mixture in a 900ml/ 1½ pint basin for 3½–4 hours.*

FOOTBALL CRAZY

4-egg all-in-one cake mixture (p. 10)—omit baking powder and bake in a 25 × 20cm/ 10 × 8in roasting tin for 45–50 minutes until firm to touch
apricot jam
decoration or gelatine icing (pp.18–19)
butter icing (p.20)
12in square cake board
food colourings: blue, yellow, green and black
nozzles: medium star
2 liquorice laces
50g/2 oz desiccated coconut
50g/2 oz chocolate dots

Split the cake in half and sandwich with jam. Cut the cake into a boot and a ball shape. Place on the board. Roll out half the decoration icing into an oblong large enough to cover the top and sides of the boot only. Cover the boot, cutting away the icing at the ankle as shown. Roll a quarter of the remaining icing into a circle and cover the football. Using the back of a knife, mark the top of the football into 5-sided pentagons as shown. Using an artist's paint brush and black food colouring, paint in the central pentagon. Divide the remaining icing in half, colour one half blue and roll out. Cut a patch to cover the ankle of the boot, a strip for the laces and a flash on the boot as shown. Colour the remaining icing yellow, roll out and cut smaller shapes to go on top of the ankle patch and flash. Cut liquorice laces and place on the cake with a bow at the ankle. Colour one half of the butter icing blue and the other half yellow. Using a star nozzle, pipe alternate coloured stripes for the sock as shown. Place chocolate dots on the sole of the boot. Colour the coconut green and sprinkle over the cake board.

KITTY THE CAT

Ideal for a birthday cake, or if you wish, pipe with chocolate butter icing for a Hallowe'en witches' cat.

20–23cm/8–9in round all-in-one cake (p.10)
raspberry jam
double quantity vanilla-flavoured butter icing (p.20)
12in round cake board
food colouring: blue
nozzle: small star
1 packet jelly sweets
1 strip liquorice
1 plastic bell (p.80)

Split the cake in half and sandwich with jam. Cut the cake as shown in the diagram. Place the horseshoe-shaped body on the board. Join the head and tail to the sides, trimming to fit and secure with a little jam. Spread the cake all over with butter icing. Reserve 4 tbsp of butter icing and colour the

remaining icing blue. Using a small star nozzle, pipe blue stars all over the cake as illustrated. Pipe a straight line of icing to mark off the cat's legs. Using vanilla icing and a small star nozzle, over-pipe the paws, the tip of the tail, the inside of the ears, and around the eyes and nose.

Place the jelly sweets on the cake for the eyes, nose and tongue. Cut the liquorice into 6 thin strips and stick into the icing around the nose for whiskers. Place a bell at the cat's neck and arrange the jelly sweets as a collar around Kitty's neck.

A DARTMOOR PONY

two 23cm/9in round all-in-one cakes (p.10) or two whisked sponge cakes (pp.12–13)
apricot jam
double quantity coffee-flavoured butter icing (p.20)
chocolate-flavoured butter icing (p.20)
12in round cake board
3 strips liquorice and 1 liquorice sweet

Sandwich the cakes together with jam. Cut out the horse's head and ear as shown in the diagram. Place the horse's head on the board. Join the ear to the head with a little butter icing. Spread the cake all over with coffee butter icing. Mark a line to show the curve of the head against the neck as shown. Put the chocolate butter icing in a greaseproof paper icing bag and snip the end. Pipe the mane along the horse's neck. Arrange the strips of liquorice on the cake to form a bridle as shown. Pipe an eye, the nostrils and mouth as shown.

SWEETIE STREET

To make 6 houses.

two all-in-one cakes (p. 10) baked in two
  23cm/9in deep square tins
raspberry jam
cornflour
1kg/2 lb decoration or gelatine
  icing (pp. 18–19)
or Whitworths fondant icing
butter icing (p. 20)
two 10in oblong cake boards
decorations as desired

Cut each cake into 2 halves (oblongs). Trim tri-angular wedges from 2 long sides of 2 oblongs to make the roofs. Place on top of the other 2 oblongs, sandwiched together with jam. Dust the work surface with cornflour. Roll out a little of the decoration, gelatine or fondant icing. Cut and trim to make six 2.5cm/1in squares. Press a cocktail stick into each one and leave to dry on greaseproof paper.

Divide the remaining decoration, gelatine or fondant icing into quarters. Roll and trim each piece to an oblong 25 × 7.5cm/10 × 3in. Thinly spread one side of each cake with jam and wrap the icing against the side, pressing and smoothing down firmly. Repeat to cover the sides of both the cakes.

Spread the roof of each house with butter icing and place the cakes on the boards. With the back of a knife, divide and mark each cake into 3 houses.

To decorate houses Use any of the following ideas. For the roof, cut shredded wheat biscuits in half or use mini shreddies to make a thatch. Or use liquorice sweets, sponge, chocolate or wafer finger biscuits, or chocolate flake bars or buttons to make a variety of roofs. Press onto the butter icing and arrange as shown.

For the windows and doors, stick fruity chews, liquorice sweets or strips onto the houses with a little butter icing. Or colour butter icing with food colouring as desired, place in greaseproof paper icing bags and snip off the ends. Pipe windows, curtains and doors as shown.

To create a garden, spread the cake boards very thinly with a little butter icing and cover with any of the following: desiccated or long thread coconut coloured green for the lawns; sprinkled-on chocolate-flavoured sugar strands or flakes, or coloured hundreds and thousands, liquorice sweets, coloured chocolate beans or sweets for pretty gardens. Divide the gardens with hedges of mini shreddies, liquorice sweets or sugar flowers and jelly sweets.

Write the names of the children and their ages onto each square of icing with a little food colouring, or pipe on the names with butter icing. Place the squares in sweets at the end of each garden or on the roofs.

COMING OF AGE

HELLO SAILOR

25cm/10in square rich fruit cake (pp.8–9)
almond paste (pp.14–15)
royal icing (p.16)
13in square cake board
food colourings: blue and brown
nozzles: no. 1 and 2 plain, small and medium star
1.25m/1¼yd dark blue ribbon, 2.5cm/1in wide
1.25m/1¼yd light blue ribbon, 1cm/½in wide

Cover the cake with almond paste and place on the board. Flat ice the top and sides of the cake and allow to dry for 24 hours.

Run-out sails and boat Trace off the templates (p.78) and follow the instructions for separate run-outs (p.26), making the icing a little thicker than usual. Place each newly completed run-out over a rolling pin to dry – this gives the sails a curve. The boat run-out is dried flat.

To decorate borders Using white icing and a medium star nozzle, pipe 2 rows of stars around the top edge of the cake and 1 row of stars around the bottom edge. Using white icing and a no. 2 nozzle, pipe the outline around the stars onto the cake board. Using blue icing and a no. 1 or no. 2 nozzle, pipe in a circular motion over the stars, so that the thread of icing circles around the point of the star and drops in a loop between each one.

Draw and cut out a 20cm/8in oval template and place on top of the cake. With an artist's paint brush outline and colour the oval pale blue. Allow to dry. Place the boat on top, followed by the sails, fixing the sails one on top of the other with a dab of icing between. Draw the rope lines with food colouring and a very fine brush. Using white icing and a star nozzle, pipe waves around the boat. Using light blue icing and a small star nozzle, make a frame of

stars around the oval shape. Using blue icing and a no. 1 nozzle, pipe the boy's name. Wrap the light and dark blue ribbons around the cake and secure with a dot of icing.

FIONA'S 18th

25cm/10in round rich fruit cake (pp.8–9)
almond paste (pp.14–15)
royal icing (p.16)
13in round cake board
food colourings: pink and green
nozzles: no. 2 plain, medium and small petal
40 medium pale pink roses (p.30)
12 tiny pale pink roses (p.30)
40 tiny deeper pink roses (p.30)
18th birthday key

Cover the cake with almond paste and place on the board. Colour one-third of the icing pale green and the remainder rose pink. To cover the side of the cake, first put green icing on the bottom half and spread with a palette knife, then put pink icing on the top half and spread with a palette knife to meet the green icing. Smooth the side with a scraper (p.17). The green and pink icings will merge into each other along the join. Allow to dry before flat icing the top of the cake with pink icing.

To decorate board Using green icing and a no. 2 nozzle, pipe a scalloped line around the board. Soften about 4 tbsp of green icing with a little egg white or water, place in a greaseproof paper icing bag, snip off the end and flood in the scallops. Allow to dry for 24 hours.

To make leaves (p.31) With green icing in a grease-proof paper icing bag, pipe leaves around the top edge of the cake and place the dry, medium pale pink roses onto the leaves while the leaves are still moist. Pipe a few leaves on the board. Colour the icing a deeper green and put into a new icing bag cut to form a smaller leaf shape. Pipe more leaves onto the board and the side of the cake, and arrange the tiny deep pink roses interspersed with the tiny pale pink roses on the smaller leaves.

Using deeper pink icing and a no. 2 nozzle, write the girl's name and place the key on top of the cake.

COMING OF AGE

25cm/10in square rich fruit cake (pp.8–9)
almond paste (pp.14–15) plus 225g/8 oz
  royal icing (p.16)
16in square cake board
nozzle: medium star
2 large modelled roses and leaves (p.32)
2.25m/2½yd gold-coloured ribbon
two 18th or 21st birthday keys

Cut the cake in half to make two 25 × 12.5cm/
10 × 5in oblongs. Cover each half with almond paste and place on the board as illustrated. Flat ice the tops and sides of the cakes. Allow to dry for 24 hours and cover with a second thin coat of icing. Allow to dry for 24 hours.

To decorate borders Using a medium star nozzle, pipe a row of shells around the bottom edge of each cake and pipe the top edges in the same way. Place a single modelled rose on each cake. Angle a bow of ribbon across the bottom corner of each cake. Wrap a piece of ribbon around each cake, securing the ribbon at the back of the cake with a spot of icing. Place a key on the top of each cake.

21st SURPRISE

20cm/8in round rich fruit cake (pp.8–9)
almond paste (pp.14–15)
royal icing (p.16)
decoration icing (p.18)
11in round cake board
food colourings: blue, yellow and pink
nozzles: no.2 plain, medium and small star
a tiny blue ribbon

Cover the cake with almond paste, place on the board and flat ice top and sides with royal icing.

To model girl's figure Colour two-thirds of the decoration icing with a little pink food colouring and form into a cone shape. Make a cut each side for the arms. Pinch and shape top to form the head and neck. Pinch in the middle of the cone to form a waist. Model the bust, soften and bend arms, and model hands and features. Put a cocktail stick up through the figure to give support. Lie the figure on greaseproof paper to dry and harden for up to 1 week. Using a fine artist's paint brush, mark in the eyes and mouth. Using a no. 1 plain nozzle and yellow icing, pipe hair onto the head and down over her shoulders.

Roll out remaining white decoration icing. Cut a 5cm/2in × 2.5cm/1in oblong for the plaque. Cut out 8 jagged triangles to look like pieces of torn paper, drape these on waxed paper over a rolling pin and leave to dry and harden for 24 hours.

To decorate border Use a medium star nozzle. Pipe shells around the top and bottom edge of the cake. With a no. 2 nozzle and deep blue icing outline the shells on top of the cake and on the board. Follow the outline using a no. 1 nozzle and pipe similar lines in yellow icing.

To decorate sides Divide the top of the cake into 8 sections, marking each with a dot. Using a small star nozzle and white icing, pipe curves of stars between the dots as illustrated and flatten points gently with a finger. Tilt cake and, with a no. 2 plain nozzle and deep blue icing, pipe dropped lines inside the curves. Pipe a second line over the stars using a lighter blue. With yellow icing and a no. 2 nozzle pipe tassels between the curves by making 3 loops.

Position the girl in the centre of the cake with a little icing. Pipe a circle of white stars around her and stand triangles of 'torn paper' into icing. Using an artist's paint brush and food colouring, write a message onto an oblong plaque and place on top of the cake with the ribbon bow.

SPECIAL CELEBRATION CAKES

SOMETHING TO CELEBRATE

25cm/10in round rich fruit cake (pp.8–9)
almond paste (optional) (pp.14–15)
1.5kg/3 lb decoration icing (p.18)
small quantity of royal icing (p.16)
12in round cake board
food colourings: pink, lilac and green
1m/1yd lilac ribbon, 1cm/½in wide
1m/1yd pink ribbon, 3mm/⅛in wide
15cm/6in lilac ribbon, 3mm/⅛in wide

Cover the cake with almond paste (if using) and place on the board. Make up 900g/2 lb of decoration icing, reserve 100g/4 oz for the top decoration and roll out the remaining icing to cover the cake.

To make top decoration Using the reserved 100g/4 oz of decoration icing, form into a small cone shape about 5cm/2in high and allow to dry on greaseproof paper until firm.

To make flowers and frills (pp.36–7) Make up a further 450g/1 lb of decoration icing and divide into 3 equal pieces. Cut one of the 3 pieces into 6 (wrap in cling film when not using) and roll each piece to an oblong 20 × 2.5cm/8 × 1in. Mark a line 6mm/¼in in from one long side and roll with a cocktail stick to frill. Brush the base of the cake with a little water and press the frill against the cake. Repeat to completely cover the base of the cake. Use another third to cut out and frill 12 large flowers using a 2.5cm/1in fluted cutter and a shell using a 6.5cm/2½in fluted cutter for the top decoration (p.37). Colour a small piece of icing (the size of a walnut) green. Press tiny pieces into oval shapes between your finger and thumb, mark a vein down the centre and twist slightly to form leaves. Make about 30 leaves. Divide the remaining icing in half, colour 1 piece pink and the other piece lilac, knead together and use to make about 45 small two-tone flowers. Allow all flowers, leaves, shell and top decoration to dry on greaseproof paper at least overnight, longer if possible.

Using an artist's paint brush and pink food colouring, lightly brush the edges of the white flowers and the edge of the cake frill. Secure all the flowers onto the cake using a little royal icing on the back of each. Secure the small two-tone flowers onto the white flowers. Place 3 completed flowers around the cone for the top decoration and evenly space 9 more around the top edge of the cake. Place a green leaf on either side of the flowers. Place 4 small two-tone flowers in a curve between each white flower on the side of the cake.

Wrap the ribbons around the cake and around the top decoration, securing with a little icing. Place the top decoration on the centre of the cake. Thread the narrow lilac ribbon through the shell and place behind the top decoration, securing in position with a little icing.

CARNATION CAKE

20cm/8in square rich fruit cake (pp.8–9)
almond paste (optional) (pp.14–15)
675g/1½ lb decoration or gelatine
   icing (pp.18–19)
royal icing (p.16)
10in square cake board
food colourings: lilac and pink
nozzles: no. 1 and 2 plain
1m/1yd heather pink ribbon
green fern

Cover the cake with almond paste (if using), place on the board and cover with 450g/1 lb decoration or gelatine icing.

To make carnations (p.33) Tint the remaining decoration or gelatine icing with pink and lilac food colourings to give the desired colour, and use the icing to make 5 carnations. Allow to dry for at least 4 hours, preferably overnight. With a dot of icing secure the ribbon diagonally up and over the 2 opposite corners of the cake. Tie 2 small ribbon bows and place on the cake with a dot of icing. Place the carnations as shown onto the centre of the cake and secure with a little royal icing. Place a small piece of green fern between each flower, fixing with a little icing.

To decorate sides and border Using royal icing and a no. 1 or no. 2 nozzle (or use a greaseproof paper icing bag and snip off the end), pipe small dots on either side of the ribbon. Pipe little flowers in rows following the line of the ribbon, by piping 5 dots in a circle with a centre dot. Pipe a row of small dots around the base of the cake. Pipe another 2 dots between every second and third dot and 1 dot between these 2 to give the lace effect.

ANNIVERSARY CAKES

SILVER WEDDING CAKE

25cm/10in square rich fruit cake (pp.8–9)
almond paste (pp.14–15)
royal icing (p.16)
13in cake board
140cm/54in narrow silver–coloured cake band
food colouring: edible silver
**nozzles: no. 1 and 2 plain, small and medium
    star**
8 large white roses (p.30)
16 silver rose leaves

Cover the cake with almond paste, place on the board and flat ice top and sides with royal icing.

To decorate board Measure 12.5cm/5in in from each side of the board. Mark with a dot of icing. Use royal icing and a no. 1 or no. 2 nozzle and pipe a curved line between these dots. Pipe a curved line from either side of the dots to the corners of the board. Repeat on each side, making sure that the lines meet at the corners. Soften a little icing with egg white or water until it just flows. Put in a greaseproof paper icing bag and snip end. Carefully fill in the curves with the soft icing. Prick out any air bubbles and leave to dry for 24 hours.

To make template for cake top Cut one 20cm/8in circle and one 20cm/8in square of paper. Fold the square in half and in half again. Fold diagonally to give a triangle and cut the right angle into a curve (see diagram). Unfold to give an equal 4-petal shape. Centre petal shape on cake top and place the circle on top again. Anchor with tiny dots of icing which can be removed when the templates are taken off. Pipe dots of icing to mark the part of the circle which lies between the petal shape. Remove the circle template. Use a no. 2 nozzle and pipe a continuous line around the whole of the petal shape. Remove the template. Pipe lines of trellis work (p.28) in the curved spaces between petals as shown in the picture. Pipe small stars around the outer edge of the trellis.

To decorate sides Matching the curve on the board, pipe a curve of marking dots on each side of the cake. Pipe lines of trellis from the top of the curve to within 6mm/¼in of the edge of the run-out.

Finish with a row of small stars around the curves. Using a no. 1 nozzle, pipe decorative edging around the run-out on the board and a matching edging inside the petal. Pipe 25 stars in the centre.

To decorate border Use a medium star nozzle and pipe 2 rows of stars on the top and side edge.

Place roses and silver leaves on the top and corners. Secure with a little icing. Wrap a silver band around the cake and secure with icing. With a fine artist's paint brush and silver food colouring paint over the '25' and the petal lines.

RUBY WEDDING CAKE

20cm/8in square rich fruit cake (pp.8–9)
almond paste (pp.14–15)
royal icing (p.16)
11in cake board
food colouring: red
nozzles: no. 1 and 2 plain, medium star, frill or ribbon
red modelled roses
green fern or silver leaves

Cover the cake with almond paste, place on the board and flat ice top and sides with royal icing.

To decorate board Follow run-out directions for the silver wedding cake. Allow to dry for 24 hours.

To decorate top Trace off and cut out the '40' template (p.78). Put in one corner of the cake and secure with a dot of icing. Using a no. 1 plain nozzle, outline the numbers with white icing. Soften a little icing with water or egg white until it just flows. Place in a greaseproof icing bag and snip end. Pipe into the outline. Allow to dry for 24 hours.

To decorate sides Using the ribbon/frill nozzle, pipe 3 curved frills (similar in size to the curves on the board) in white icing on each side.

To decorate border Using a medium star nozzle, pipe swirls on the top edge (p.24).

Red piping There is always a danger of red colour bleeding into the white, so the cake must be dry and the red colouring only piped a day or so before serving. Using a no. 1 plain nozzle, outline the numbers. Tilt the cake and pipe drop-curved lines on the sides just touching the top of the frill. Pipe pretty bows at the top of each curve. Pipe decorative edging around run-out on the cake board.

With a little icing fix the red roses and fern on top of the cake.

GOOD LUCK IN YOUR NEW JOB

**two all-in-one cakes (p. 10) baked in two
28 × 18cm/11 × 7in Swiss roll tins
apricot jam
1kg/2 lb decoration icing (p. 18)
or Whitworths fondant icing
12in square cake board
food colourings: brown, yellow and orange**

Sandwich the cakes with jam and place on the board. Thinly spread the top and sides with jam. For the newspaper, colour 75g/3 oz of the decoration or fondant icing orange. Roll out and trim to a 20cm/8in square. Fold in 3 and leave to dry on greaseproof paper. Colour 50g/2 oz of the decoration or fondant icing yellow, reserve a quarter and roll the remaining icing into a handle shape. Put half a cocktail stick into each end of the handle and leave to dry overnight. Colour remaining icing brown. Roll out and trim to an oblong 35 × 30cm/

14 × 12in. Cut two 30 × 2.5cm/12 × 1in straps, and place the rest of the icing over the top and sides of the cake. Place the straps across the cake as shown and press down lightly. Use the back of a knife to mark a line along the centre of the sides of the cake.

Roll out the yellow decoration or fondant icing and cut out one 2.5cm/1in circle. Cut out a keyhole shape from the centre. Also cut out four 4cm/1½in circles, cut each in half and shape to form corner pieces as shown. Brush the back of each corner piece and keyhole piece with a little water and place on the cake. Roll the yellow icing trimmings into initials and 2 small rolls for combination locks. Brush with a little water and place on the cake. Place the newspaper at an angle to the right-hand side of the cake. Using brown food colour, paint 'Financial Times' and an appropriate message onto the newspaper! Paint screws on each side of the corner pieces and paint the combination numbers onto the locks. Secure the handle to the cake with a cocktail stick.

BOUQUET OF BEST WISHES

two all-in-one cakes (p.10) or whisked sponge cakes (pp.12–13) baked in 32 × 22 cm/ 12½ × 8½ in Swiss roll tins
apricot jam
rich butter cream (p.21)
decoration icing (p.18) or Whitworths fondant icing
13in square cake board
food colourings: pink, violet, yellow and green
ribbon bow

Sandwich the cakes together with rich butter cream. Cut into a bouquet shape by rounding the top 2 corners and tapering the bouquet to a point as shown. (Use the cake trimmings for a trifle!) Place the cake on the board and spread the top and sides thinly with jam. Divide the decoration or fondant icing into 4. Colour 1 piece pale pink, roll out to an oblong 20 × 15cm/8 × 6in and cut into eight 2.5cm/1in strips. Place the strips 2.5cm/1in apart on the cake as shown, trimming to fit. Repeat with another piece of white icing, to form the stripes of pink and white icing. Cut a flat 5cm/2in piece for a label and allow to dry on greaseproof paper. Roll out a further strip of white icing about 40 × 5cm/ 16 × 2in, wrap around the curved side of the cake and trim.

Divide the remaining icing into 5 pieces and colour each piece differently – bright pink, pale pink, lilac, yellow and green. Roll out each piece and cut out shapes as desired with a cocktail cutter or a 5cm/2in fluted pastry cutter. Make small cuts around the large and small circles to divide them into petals. Arrange 5 heart shapes in a circle with a yellow centre to make a flower. Arrange flowers, overlapping slightly, to completely cover space.

Place a ribbon bow on top. With food colouring and an artist's paint brush write 'best wishes' on the label and tuck it under the bow.

MOVING HOUSE OR RETIREMENT

A COUNTRY COTTAGE

**all-in-one cake (p.10) baked in 23cm/9in deep
  square tin**
raspberry jam
double quantity butter icing (p.20)
10in square cake board
**food colourings: green, brown, pink and
  yellow**
50g/2 oz desiccated coconut
8 shredded wheat biscuits
4 greaseproof paper icing bags

Cut the cake into 2 halves (oblongs). Trim triangular wedges from 2 long sides of 1 oblong to make a roof and place on top of the other oblong. Sandwich with jam. Place the cake to one side of the cake board and cover the top and sides of the cake with butter icing. Divide the remaining butter icing into 4 small basins and colour green, brown, pink and yellow. Place each colour into a greaseproof paper icing bag and snip off the ends. Using brown icing, pipe 4 windows and a door onto the front of the cottage and pipe a winding stone path from the front door to the edge of the board. With green icing pipe a rose tree around the door and over the window, using pink icing to pipe dots for roses around the door and a few around the base of the cottage. Spread remaining green icing thinly over the cake board. Colour the coconut green and scatter over the board taking care not to cover the path. Split 4 shredded wheat biscuits in half and place on the roof as shown. Cut the remaining biscuits into 4 strips and cut each strip in half. Cut 1 strip across its width and place 1 piece over the door of the cottage. Place the remaining strips around the edge of the board as a fence and secure with icing if necessary. Using yellow and pink icings, pipe little flowers amongst the grass.

★ *This cake could also be made with a rich fruit cake mixture, covered with almond paste and royal or decoration icing.*

ONE MAN WENT TO MOW

**4-egg all-in-one cake mixture (p. 10)—omit
baking powder and bake in a 25 × 20cm/
10 × 8in roasting tin for 45–50 minutes until
firm to touch**
raspberry jam
vanilla-flavoured butter icing (p.20)
**225g/8 oz decoration or gelatine icing
(pp. 18–19)**
or 1 packet Whitworths fondant icing
12in square cake board
**food colourings: pink, green, brown, blue and
orange**
100g/4 oz desiccated coconut
1 box chocolate sticks

Sandwich the cake with jam and place on the board.
Cover with butter icing. Make the grass by colouring the coconut green, reserve half and colour the
remaining coconut a deeper green. Mark out strips
across the cake and sprinkle with alternate rows of
light and dark green coconut.
To make figure (pp.34–5) Use 50g/2 oz of decoration or fondant icing to model the man and leave to
dry on greaseproof paper overnight.
To make lawn mower and path Colour a small piece
of decoration or fondant icing orange and form into
a 4cm/1½in square. Colour 50g/2 oz of icing
brown, make into a small square and place on top

of the orange mower. Roll a very thin piece of
white icing into a long rope, curve in half, and lay
the rope on greaseproof paper to dry overnight.
Make steps, stepping stones, pebbles and a vege-
table patch in brown icing. Place on the cake.
To make pond Colour a little decoration or fondant
icing blue and roll out to make the pond. Place on
one corner of the cake and surround with pebbles.
To make flowers Using a little white and a little pink
icing, roll out 10 small circles, slightly varying in
size. With the point of a knife, make 5 cuts around
each circle to form petals. Paint yellow dots of food
colouring in the centre of each. Place the flowers
around the pond amongst the grass as shown.
To make fence Arrange chocolate sticks around the
edge of the cake, cutting the sticks in three to form
the bars of the fence.

Use icing trimmings to make the vegetables and
bushes as shown. Model tree shapes and skewer
with a cocktail stick. Allow to dry until firm before
arranging on the cake as illustrated.

Just before serving stand the man on the cake,
secure the figure with a little butter icing and rest
the handle of the lawn mower on the base of the
mower and against the man's hands.

MOTHER'S DAY AND FATHER'S DAY

WITH LOVE TO MUM

**18–20cm/7–8in round whisked sponge cake
(pp.12–13)**
3 tbsp lemon curd
**300ml/½ pint double cream with vanilla
essence and icing sugar to taste or
vanilla-flavoured rich butter cream
(p.21)**
**marzipan or almond paste primroses, leaves
and daffodils (p.33)**

Sandwich the cake with lemon curd. Place on a pretty serving plate or cake board. Put the double cream (if using) in a small basin and lightly whip until it just holds its shape. Spread the top of the cake with half-whipped cream or butter cream. Using a round-ended knife or small palette knife, swirl cream from centre outwards in a circular pattern. Put remaining cream or butter cream in an icing bag fitted with a medium star nozzle. Pipe a border around the edge of the cake and decorate the centre with primroses, leaves and daffodils. Store in the refrigerator for up to 2 days.

DAD'S FAVOURITE BREW

**3-egg quantity of all-in-one cake recipe – omit
  baking powder (p.10)**
chocolate-flavoured butter icing (p.20)
vanilla-flavoured butter icing (p.20)
7in round thin cake board
a little decoration icing (p.18)
  or a little Whitworths fondant icing
  or white cardboard
2 cocktail sticks

Line the base and grease the sides of 2 clean, dry
225g/8oz coffee tins, or two 12.5cm/5in greased and
lined cake tins. Divide the cake mixture between
the tins. Bake for 35–40 minutes. When cooked the
cakes should feel firm to touch and have begun to
shrink from the sides of the tin. Turn onto a wire
rack and allow to cool.

To decorate cake Cut a 2.5-cm/1-in thick slice from
the top of the cake and cut into a handle shape.
Sandwich remaining cakes together with half the
vanilla-flavoured butter icing. Place on the cake
board. Reserve 3 tbsp chocolate-flavoured butter
icing. Spread the rest of the butter icing carefully
onto the side of the cake and handle. Place the
handle against side and secure with cocktail sticks.
Roughly spread remaining vanilla-flavoured butter
icing on top of the cake, allowing a little to 'spill'
down the side.

Roll out decoration or fondant icing and cut out
an oval plaque, or cut one out from the cardboard.
Place remaining chocolate-flavoured butter icing
into a paper icing bag, snip end and pipe a message
onto the plaque. Position on the side of the cake.
Keeps well for up to 5–6 days.

BOX AND BASKET CAKES

A BASKET OF ROSES

18cm/7in round rich fruit cake (pp.8–9)
almond paste (pp.14–15)
royal icing (p.16)
9in round cake board
food colourings: pink, red, yellow, orange
and brown
nozzles: no. 3 plain, basket, large star
1m/1yd pink ribbon
modelling paste (p.32)
46cm/18in cane or wire for handle

Cover the cake with almond paste and place on the cake board. Colour the royal icing with a few drops of yellow colouring and a drop or two of brown colouring to make the icing cane coloured. Flat ice the top of the cake only. Cover the side with basket work piping (p.29). Using a large star nozzle, pipe a shell edging around the top and bottom edge of the basket.

To make roses (p.32) Model large roses, mixing modelling paste with food colourings to give as many different shades as desired. Place the roses on top of the basket, securing each with a little royal icing.

To make handle Cut the ribbon in half, wind one half around the cane or wire, secure with a dot of icing and push the ends of the cane or wire into the top of the cake. Tie a bow on the handle with the remaining ribbon.

BOX OF SWEETS

20cm/8in square rich fruit cake (pp.8–9)
almond paste (optional) (pp.14–15)
1kg/2 lb decoration icing (p.18)
225g/8 oz royal icing (p.16)
10in and 8in thin square cake boards
food colourings: blue, pink, green, yellow and
orange
food flavourings: strawberry, raspberry,
lemon, orange, peppermint and chocolate
nozzles: no. 1 plain, small star
½m/½yd white ribbon, 2.5cm/1in wide

Cut the cake into an oblong 20 × 12.5cm/8 × 5in. (Serve the remaining portion separately – cover with icing if you wish.) Cut the small cake board into an oblong 20 × 12.5cm/8in × 5in for the lid. Cover the cake with almond paste (if using). Place the cake on the larger board.

Colour 450g/1 lb of decoration icing blue, reserve 100g/4 oz and use the rest of the icing to cover the cake. Cover the white side of the 'lid' with the remaining blue icing. With the edge of a clean plastic ruler, press diagonal lines across the sides of the cake and on the lid. Colour two-thirds of the royal icing blue. Using a small star nozzle, pipe shells around the top and bottom edges of the cake. Stand the lid on a basin and pipe shells around the edge. Colour the remaining royal icing pink. Using a no. 1 nozzle, pipe forget-me-nots at the points where the diagonal lines meet. Pipe a darker pink dot for the centre.

To make sweets Divide up 450g/1 lb white decoration icing, flavour each piece and colour as appropriate. Roll out and shape with cocktail cutters or press into petit fours moulds. Place the sweets on top of the cake. Place a strip of ribbon across the lid, tie a bow and secure to the lid with royal icing as shown.

EASTER CAKES

EASTER BUNNIE

**two 20cm/8in round all-in-one cakes (p.10)
or two whisked sponge cakes (pp.12–13)
raspberry or strawberry jam
double quantity vanilla-flavoured butter
icing (p.20)
16in cake board
food colourings: pink and green
175g/6 oz desiccated coconut
cocktail sticks
1 packet marshmallows
6 glacé cherries
angelica**

Cut each cake as shown in diagram 1. Sandwich 2 bodies, 2 heads and 2 tails together with a little jam. Stand the body upright on the cake board. Colour two-thirds of the icing with pink food colouring. Spread a little icing onto the cut side of the head and press against the body as shown in diagram 2. Cover the bunnie completely with pink and vanilla icing, using a medium star nozzle to pipe as illustrated. Cover each ear and tail with vanilla icing. Coat ears and tail in desiccated coconut. Place ears at slightly different angles on top of the head and secure with cocktail sticks. Position tail at the end with a blob of icing. Cut 1 marshmallow in half for the eyes. Cut the glacé cherries into quarters and place one quarter on each marshmallow eye. Secure in position with a little icing. Cut 2 marshmallows in half for the feet and cut 1 in half for the nose.

With a pair of wetted scissors cut a cross in each remaining marshmallow and place a quarter glacé cherry in the top of each marshmallow flower. Cut angelica leaves for each flower and 6 short strips for whiskers – push into icing around the nose. Add a few drops of green food colouring to remaining coconut and stir well until evenly coloured. Scatter around the bunnie and arrange marshmallow flowers around the cake.

SIMNEL CAKE

**rich fruit cake mixture sufficient for an
18–20cm/7–8in round cake (pp.8–9)
675g/1½ lb almond paste or marzipan
(pp.14–15)
apricot jam
9–10in round cake board
50cm/20in yellow ribbon**

Roll out one-third of the almond paste to a circle the size of the cake tin. Make the cake mixture. Place half into the prepared cake tin. Top with almond paste and the remaining cake mixture. Bake as for rich fruit cake method. When cold, turn out, remove paper lining and store in a tin.

To decorate cake Brush the top of the cake with warmed sieved apricot jam. Roll out half of the remaining almond paste to a circle the size of the cake. Place on top, press down lightly and crimp the edge between your finger and thumb. Using the back of a knife, mark off the top of the cake in diagonal lines to form a lattice. Lightly brown the cake under a moderate grill. Put on the cake board. Use remaining almond paste to make 5 chicks and 6 bunnies (p.35). Brush the base of each with a little apricot jam and place around the edge of the cake. Wrap the ribbon around the cake and tie with a bow.

1

2

A CHRISTMAS CAROL

25cm/10in square rich fruit cake (pp.8–9)
almond paste (pp.14–15)
royal icing (p.16)
13in square cake board
food colourings: red, green, black, brown and
yellow
nozzles: no. 1 and 2 plain, medium star
20 bells (p.26)

Cover the cake with almond paste and place on the cake board. Flat ice the top and sides with royal icing.

To decorate board Colour 4 tbsp of icing green. Using a no. 2 plain nozzle and green icing, pipe the outlines of 3 holly leaves on each corner of the cake board. Change to white icing and, with a no. 2 nozzle, pipe a line around the edge of the cake board as illustrated. Mix 6 tbsp white icing with a little water or egg white until it just flows. Carefully spoon onto the cake board and allow to flood out to the white piped line, using a cocktail stick to ease it up to the outline of the holly and being careful not to overrun the leaves. Leave to dry for 24 hours.

To make carol singers Trace off the templates on p.79 and follow the directions for the contour run-outs on p.26. Add red colouring to 3 tbsp of royal icing and pipe the outline of the coat onto waxed paper. Using half of the red icing add sufficient egg white or water to give a whipped cream consistency. Put into a greaseproof paper icing bag. Snip end. Fill in the coat, making thicker strokes to show the folds of the coat and the arms. Using green icing and the same method, make the green coat. Dry for 24–48 hours. Peel the paper away gently and position the red and green coats on the cake, fixing with a little icing underneath. Using a

fine artist's paint brush and food colouring, outline the face, eyes, mouth and hair. With white icing of piping consistency, and using a ribbon/frill nozzle (p.36), pipe the little girl's petticoat. Take 2 tbsp of white icing and mix with black colouring – with a no. 1 nozzle pipe the buttons, decorative lines and hat to complete the girl's red outfit. Also with black icing pipe the wrought-iron lamp, the outline of the board and write Merry Christmas. Use an artist's fine brush and yellow colour to paint in the lamp light. Mix 2 tbsp of white icing with brown colouring and, with a small star nozzle, pipe fur on the girl's green coat and hat. Fold tiny pieces of paper for carol books and position with a dot of icing. Pipe a few green strokes around the lamp post and add a little white icing around the girls for snow.

To decorate borders Using white royal icing and a star nozzle, make 2 rows around the top edge as shown in the illustration. With red icing of piping consistency pipe loops around the border and repeat with the green icing. Fix the bells to the corners and middle of each side with a little icing. Use a no. 2 nozzle and white icing to pipe a line of dots over the join at the base of the cake.

FESTIVE GARLAND

20cm/8in all-in-one cake baked in a ring mould (p.10)
4 tbsp apricot or raspberry jam
vanilla-flavoured butter icing (p.20) or royal icing (p.16)
10in round cake board
14 Christmas roses (p.33)
20 holly leaves and berries (p.35)
50cm/20in red ribbon

Split the cake in half and sandwich together with jam. Place on the cake board and cover with butter or royal icing. Peak the icing with a round-ended knife. Press roses, holly leaves and berries onto the cake, leaving a 5cm/2in space at the top of one side for the bow. When the icing has dried tie the ribbon into a bow and place on the cake. The cake will keep for up to 5 or 6 days in a cake tin.

THREE SMALL CAKES

15cm/6in round rich fruit cake (pp.8–9)
almond paste (pp. 14–15)
royal icing (p.16)
8in silver board

Cover the cake with almond paste and place on the cake board. Flat ice the top and sides with royal icing.

CHRISTMAS CANDLES

food colourings: yellow, green, red and edible gold
nozzles: no. 1 and 2 plain, medium and small star
4 piped Christmas roses (p.30)

To decorate top Soften about 6 tbsp royal icing with egg white or water until the icing just flows. Put 2 tbsp of icing in a separate bowl and add a drop of yellow colouring and cover. Use white icing of piping consistency with a no. 2 nozzle and outline the board. Carefully flood the board with the softened icing. To make the holly design, dip a cocktail stick into green food colouring and place on the wet, iced board. Pull gently to form short curved lines, then pull away slightly at points on

either side to form the points of the leaf. Repeat at regular intervals around the board. Dip the cocktail stick into red colouring, drain off as much colour as possible and just lightly touch the wet icing with dots to form berries. Allow the border to dry for 24 hours before icing the side of the cake.

To decorate side of cake Mark off the edge of the cake into 8 equal sections with a dot of icing. Using a no. 2 plain nozzle and yellow royal icing, tilt the cake and pipe curved lines around the sides.

To make candles and scroll Trace off and cut out the templates on p.78 and place on the cake. Use a no. 2 plain nozzle and white royal icing and outline the scroll on top of the cake. Flood in with softened white icing. Using a no. 2 plain nozzle and yellow royal icing, pipe an outline of candles and flame. Soften a little yellow icing with egg white or water until it just flows. Flood in the candles. Allow to dry for 24 hours. When dry, pipe in drips with yellow icing. Use an artist's fine paint brush with yellow food colouring to paint streaks of radiating light and a red centre to the flame. Use gold food colouring to paint 'greetings' onto the scroll. Pipe leaves directly onto the cake (p.31) using green royal icing. Place 4 Christmas roses on the leaves.

To decorate borders Use a medium star nozzle with white royal icing to pipe alternating swirls around

the top edge of the cake. Change to a smaller star nozzle, repeating design around the bottom edge. With a no. 1 nozzle and yellow icing, outline large swirls on the inside edge of the top border.

ROBIN CAKE

**food colourings: red, green, brown and
  yellow**
nozzles: no. 2 plain and medium star
1m/1 yd red ribbon

Allow flat icing to dry for at least 24 hours before painting the robin on top.

To paint robin Trace the robin template (p.78) onto greaseproof paper and cut out. Place on the cake and anchor with a small weight. Using an artist's fine paint brush and brown food colouring lightly paint an outline. Lift off the template and paint in the robin's features with food colourings using light strokes of the brush.

To decorate borders Using a medium star nozzle, pipe 2 rows of stars around the top edge and 1 row around the base of the cake.

Pipe Merry Christmas Use a no. 2 plain nozzle with white royal icing. Allow to dry for 2–4 hours. Using red and yellow colourings with an almost dry fine paint brush, paint over the writing with light strokes to give a toned effect as illustrated.

SKI SCENE

**food colouring: green, brown, red and black
plastic sledge and figures
cocktail sticks**

Spread a little more royal icing on top of the cake and down over the side as illustrated. Peak icing with a round-ended knife and sprinkle with granulated sugar to add sparkle. Place the sledge and figures on the cake.

To make Christmas trees Put a little white royal icing down one side of a greaseproof paper icing bag. Fill the bag with green-coloured royal icing. Snip the ends to form a broad point (p.31). Pipe leaves against the side of the cake, pulling the point of the leaf away from the cake. Start by piping the longest row at the base of each tree, overlapping shorter rows to form a pointed tree. Pipe 4 trees around the cake. Brush tree trunks with a little food colouring. Pipe another 4 trees onto waxed paper and allow to dry for 24 hours. When dry, carefully sandwich trees into pairs with a little icing and a cocktail stick between each pair. Allow to dry for 2–3 hours. Press into top of the cake.

To make snowmen Fill a paper icing bag with white royal icing and snip end. Pipe large rounded bulbs onto waxed paper. Allow to dry for 2–3 hours. Pipe a smaller bulb on top for the head. Allow to dry completely. Decorate using a fine paint brush and food colouring. Place on the cake.

THE CHRISTMAS CHOIR

**20–23cm/8–9in round rich fruit cake (pp.8–9)
or golden Christmas cake (p.13)
almond paste (pp.14–15)
1kg/2 lb decoration or gelatine icing
(pp.18–19)
10–11in round cake board
50cm/20in red ribbon
a little royal icing (p.16)**

Cover the cake with almond paste and place on the board. Cover with 550g/1¼ lb decoration or gelatine icing. Divide remaining icing in half. Use one piece to make the choir boys and robin (p.34) and the other piece to make holly leaves, berries and a lantern (pp.34–5). Using a little royal icing on the back of each, stick holly leaves and berries around the top edge of the cake. Spread a little royal icing in a small patch on top of the cake and stand the choir boys and robin in a row. Place the lantern on a cocktail stick and push gently into the cake. If you wish, pipe greetings onto the cake with royal icing. Wrap ribbon around the cake and secure ends with a little royal icing. Store in a cake tin.

FATHER CHRISTMAS AND HIS TREE

**20cm/8in square all-in-one cake (p.10)
or rich fruit cake (pp.8–9)
apricot jam
almond paste (optional) (pp.14–15)
or butter icing (p.20)
1kg/2 lb decoration or gelatine icing
(pp.18–19)
two 9in square cake boards
food colourings: red, green, yellow and blue
icing sugar
coloured and silver cake balls
chocolate sticks
glacé icing (p.21)**

Sandwich the all-in-one cake with jam. Cut the cake as shown in the diagram. Place the largest triangle onto the cake board. Place the other 2 triangles, sides together, on the other board to form another large triangle, sandwiching with jam. Cover the top and sides of the cakes with almond paste (if using) or spread with butter icing. Reserve 100g/4 oz of the decoration icing. Cut the remainder in half and colour one half green and the other red.

Father Christmas Reserve a small piece of red icing for the arms. Roll out the remaining red icing to a triangle large enough to cover the top and sides of the cake, drape over and smooth evenly. Trim the sides. Mix a tiny piece of red icing with a little white icing to make a pale pink colour. From the pink icing form 2 hands and a 2.5cm/1in round face, brush with water and position on the cake. Roll the reserve piece of red icing into a strip for the arms, cut in half, brush with a little water and place on the cake.

Roll out the white icing. Using a 6.5cm/2½in round fluted pastry cutter, cut out a large circle. Using a 2.5cm/1in round fluted pastry cutter, cut out a small circle towards the top of the large circle to form the hair and beard. Brush the back of the icing with water and place over the face on the cake. Place the small circle at the point of the cake for a pom-pom. Cut out about 8 small circles and cut in half. Brush each half with a little water and place around the bottom edge of the cake and over the arms to form cuffs. Cut 1 circle into 8 triangles and

place down the centre of the cake as buttons. Using an artist's paint brush and food colourings, paint on Father Christmas's face. Using tiny pieces of white icing, roll out a moustache and eyebrows.

Christmas tree Roll half the green icing into 3 strips the depth of the cake by about 22cm/8½ in long. Place 1 strip against each side of the cake and press the joins together. Roll out the remaining icing and, using a large pastry cutter, cut out about 15 circles. Cut the circles in half and place on the cake. Start at the bottom edge, overlapping slightly as illustrated.

Colour the glacé icing yellow, place in a grease-proof paper icing bag, snip off the end, and pipe ribbons on the presents and curly lines as garlands on the tree. Stick silver and coloured balls onto the garlands. Cut the chocolate sticks to fit the tree trunk. Dip the point of a knife into icing sugar and lightly place on the tips of the tree branches, as snow.

TEMPLATES